BET ON YOURSELF

HOW TO BUILD UNSHAKABLE CONFIDENCE, TUNE OUT THE NOISE, AND RISE TO THE OCCASION

CHRIS MUELLER

THANK YOU

First and foremost, I would like to thank you for purchasing this book. Because of your love for reading and desire to learn, you're impacting more than just yourself, *you're impacting the world*.

Did you know that there are around 750 million adults across the globe who are illiterate?

Reading is a practice that can drastically change the quality your life, and can improve the cycle of poverty, which is a serious problem.

When I came to understand how lucky I am, simply because I know how to read, I was driven to try and spark change and provide possibility and hope for those who aren't as fortunate as you and me.

I honestly do not believe I'd be where or who I am today, without my habit of reading books. I truly believe that teaching literacy can open the door to limitless opportunites for millions of people.

With that being said, the proceeds from this book will go towards helping people around the world *learn how to read*. Your purchase of this book will help illiterate individuals become literate!

This book is dedicated to you. To your mission, to your vision, and to the decision you're about to make to always **Bet On Yourself** from this day forward.

Thank you.

BTB INTRODUCTION

n this book, I'll share with you, some of the most influential tactics I've used that have drastically changed my life. The ideas and perspectives I provide incorporate the key points that I find myself constantly reverting back to in my career and personal life. It's a simple, yet profound idea, and a declaration I've used to summarize the attitudes I've laid out in this book.

In order to maximize your time reading this material, I encourage you to grab a pen. It has always helped me to be able to jot down notes, and underline concepts that stand out to me while I read, so I can refer back to them later on. I also keep a notes section on my phone, full of key points I learn as I read. I often refer back to this when I need it most.

Once you finish the book, I hope you walk away with a refined hunger and new perspective of enthusiasm towards the process required to collide your dreams with your reality.

Everything in life circles back around to a universal truth for anyone relentlessly chasing their dreams. When you feel alone, when you come across challenges, and as you shape your own perspective through personal experiences, it's vital that you always remember to have your own back. No one wants your dreams more than you do. So you must ignore the naysayers, and make a commitment to yourself. To believe in yourself when nobody else does. To always *Bet On Yourself.*

WHAT IS BTB?

BTB stands for Be the Best, and it's a *lifestyle* that encompasses 10 tactics to optimize performance and experience success. Each tactic is written with purpose and intention to inspire you to make the most out of what you have, to maximize every day, and to drive you to new levels of production so that you can accomplish what you desire most.

The 10 tactics cultivate this concept and are intended to encourage you to block out distractions, eliminate your doubt, and work diligently towards maximizing your potential. My hope is that this book ignites your desire to become the best version of yourself, and that you begin living the BTB lifestyle and learn what it means to truly bet on yourself, so you can begin your growth journey and experience the joy that success brings.

Every person has a different story, their own experiences, and perspectives through which they view the world and lead their lives. In this book, I'll be sharing with you some of my most valuable experiences, and some of the most influential lessons I've learned that have shaped my unique journey.

MY STORY

Anyone who knows me would tell you that I'm an absolutely relentless competitor. In my earliest memories as a kid, no matter what I was playing. Whether it was soccer, baseball, basketball, or wrestling—I was always *that* kid who *hated* to lose. I would cry like a baby and throw outrageous temper tantrums anytime I didn't win. It was a problem, to say the least.

When I was nine, I made the choice to put all of my attention towards one sport. Even though I enjoyed other sports, the decision was easy for me. It was always going to be soccer. From there on, the game took over the vast majority of my life and made up most of the experiences that have molded me into who I am today. The victories, losses, and lessons I've learned on the football pitch have shaped me, refined me, and allowed me to write this book for you today.

Growing up, I was raised by my mom and dad. However, when I was 13, they decided to get a divorce. In spite of the problems that arose with my parents, they never let their personal relational problems interfere with their love or support of me and my brothers, which I'm very grateful for. My parents decided to separate for a number of different reasons, and the split up between them was hard for me and my brothers. Without diving into it in great detail, their divorce and the experiences that followed because of it, taught me early on, some of the hardest realities I've had to face to date.

Despite how difficult they were, I've grown to be grateful for those tough times, for they have shaped my character. They allowed me to grow as an individual and taught me to take full accountability for my life. I needed to take responsibility for where I was and, more importantly, for where I was going. Regardless of what had happened outside of my control, I made the choice that I wasn't going to let life happen to me, but rather to make it happen *for* me.

I came to understand from an early age that it was vital to not let a situation that was out of my control, determine my destiny. Being hit by the hard reality that life isn't always sunshine and rainbows, became a turning point for me during my teenage years. I learned how to push through hard times, and keep my eyes focused on my end goal, even if it felt like the world around me was falling apart. I learned that my parents had their own problems to work through. I, alone, was ultimately responsible for achieving my dreams. No one was going to do it for me.

Taking responsibility for my life has been a principle that has proven itself useful on multiple occasions throughout my early years. I dedicate the majority of the successes in my life so far to the experiences and challenges I faced growing up. They molded my character and helped me create the lifestyle now known as #BTB.

My journey, which led me to where I am today has been full of ups and downs. My time spent in college was invaluable and its impact on my life cannot be put into words. Going to a University and playing college soccer as a 17-year-old pushed me to mature in every area of my life. It was yet another episode where tough lessons and harsh realities truly tested my strength and willingness to get out of my comfort zone. I experienced personal growth in a variety of ways.

Facing difficulties in my studies, having problems understanding my coach, wanting more than I was being given, maturing as a man, and trying to find the balance in the lifestyle of a student-athlete, were all part of the equation. However, I knew that playing college ball was going to have to be my steppingstone if I wanted to get to the pros.

It was at school where I came to the *true* realization that I could achieve my lifelong dream of playing professional soccer, so long as I increased my commitment to improving my game. If and only if I devoted myself to my faith, and to a process of consistent growth and constant improvement. That was the only way I would be able to make my dream a reality.

My first two years at the University of Wisconsin-Madison were the toughest to say the least. We finished both my freshman and sophomore seasons near the bottom of the Big Ten standings. After my sophomore year, I was in a bad place mentally and was looking for answers. I knew I had the capability to elevate my game, but I just couldn't quite sort out what was going on upstairs, between the ears. I'm a man of faith, and I know that God works in mysterious ways. Well let's just say that he worked his magic at a time when I needed it most.

I remember on one random day, I was in the treatment room, when one of my trainers, Mitch Toda, handed me a book. I picked it up and look at the title. *"Mind Gym: An Athlete's Guide to Inner Excellence,"* by Gary Mack. I wasn't sure why he gave it to me, but I knew I was desperate for change. I needed something, anything, to have a better junior season and take my team to the championship.

Bottom line is, I took a leap of faith, and even though I was definitely not a fan of reading at the time, I read the book. Well, that leap of faith happened to be the best jump I've ever taken. God really had my back on that one.

When my junior year came around, my newly framed mindset led to several changes in my preparation. I began staying after training to do extra work. I showed up earlier than everyone else and spent extra time in the gym. I stopped going out and partying and really dialed into perfecting my craft, using that time to watch and analyze film. Because of my commitment to consistent practice, fine discipline, good decisions, patience, and efficient habits, I led my team to the first outright Big Ten Championship in our school's history. That's right. We made history! And I broke countless individual records along the way.

This may have been one of the most important lesson I've learned in my life. What was the best part about that experience? Receiving and lifting the trophy? No. Getting a Big Ten Championship ring? Nope. How about earning All-American accolades and getting drafted in the top 10? No, not that either. The best part was what I had learned, and who I became, firsthand through my own experience. One of the most valuable teachings life has to offer: you reap what you sow. You get out what you put in. And I had experienced the beauty of this universal law in my own life.

From that moment forward, I went from a substitute, role player to leaving a legacy as the only two-time All-American in the school's history. All after making the conscious decision to read one little book. One that I didn't even buy, but someone gave me as a gift. This was when I realized the power that books and expanding our knowledge really has.

Fast forward to the moment I started writing this book. I actually began writing it during my rookie year at Orlando City in the MLS. I was motivated after getting drafted and proving to myself that it *could* be done. All of the people that told me if I played college soccer, I wouldn't play pro, were officially proved wrong. And that was *very satisfying*.

In the pages ahead, I'm going to share and teach you the BTB concept and its principles. These are the methods I've gathered through my experiences that have led me to achieving my childhood dreams. The information that you will find throughout this book has come from many people who are the best of the best in their relative fields. I've combined and collaborated some of their teachings with my own thoughts and learnings.

BTB ISN'T JUST A SLOGAN OR AN ACRONYM; IT'S A WAY OF LIFE.

- It's a conscious lifestyle that works towards becoming *the best version of yourself.*

- It's a combination of vision, passion, desire, habits, confidence, self-belief, sacrifice, gratitude, and execution.

- BTB helps you defy limitations, maximize your potential, and gives you the best possible chance of living the life you desire.

- BTB is about trusting the process; a process that includes but is not limited to making mistakes, failing, and applying the principles you learn along the way.

- BTB isn't an overnight promise or a get-rich-quick scheme. It's a dedication to years and years of grinding and working towards the things you ultimately want out of life.

- Living the BTB lifestyle means making conscious decisions to take control and hold yourself accountable. It's when you assume full responsibility and take ownership for where you are and where you're going.

- The BTB lifestyle requires you to increase your self-awareness and intentionally make an effort to learn from your life experiences in order to reshape your perspective.

Committing to BTB is when you accept the massive amount of action required to accomplish your wildest dreams and go for it anyways. Because you're striving to BE THE BEST! Nothing worth having has ever come easy, and before you can win, you have to first step into the game, then play it to the best of your ability.

Not only is BTB a methodology for working hard to create the life you desire, but towards the end of the book, you will learn how to cultivate joy and be present in the process of becoming great. Principles that you can apply *right now*. I'm going to reveal to you how to remain focused on your long-term goals, while also absorbing the beauty in the current moment.

Although we're working towards creating a better future, that doesn't mean we should fall into the trap of destination-oriented happiness. That's when we feel that we'll be happy only AFTER we achieve something in the future. Your meaning and value are not tied to the things you accomplish and achieve. True value is found in those who live life with a heart full of happiness and mind that is at peace, all while aspiring to achieve greatness. That in itself is the recipe to live an empowering life, because any success that comes without true fulfillment is a failure.

I'm beyond excited to share my thoughts and experiences with you. I invite you on this journey to not only adopt a process to maximize your life and your potential, but to also help you foster enjoyment in the process. The day-to-day lives that we have the privilege to live in this very moment are blessed. Let's get started!

> **"Yesterday is gone and tomorrow has yet to come. All we have is today, let us begin."** —Mother Teresa

LEARN FROM
THE BEST

Regardless of your chosen field, your goals, or your profession, you will always have the capability to learn. The questions you need to ask yourself are: Am I open minded enough to adopt a new perspective? Am I willing to risk looking silly by failing? It takes a lot of willpower to tear down the wall of pride and ignorance and leave yourself vulnerable to the possibility of being humiliated by failure. It takes a ton of courage to go against the grain and fight for what you believe in.

It takes courage to shoot for the stars, even when you're among others who can't see past the clouds.

You'll be taking a risk, surely. But let's be honest. Is there really any other way to do it? We live in a world of infinite opportunity and limitless abundance. Why would we play it safe if there's a possibility that we CAN achieve our dreams? In the wise words of my Wisconsin soccer head coach, John Trask, "is the risk worth the reward?" This is a question I constantly ask myself when making decisions. In context, is the risk of a making a mistake or messing up, worth the reward of actually achieving your goals and living out your dream? Applying the BTB approach to your life requires that you refrain from closing your mind and open yourself up to the inherent risks of *going all in*.

Having the hunger to constantly improve is an advantage. It can be the secret ingredient to your unfinished recipe for accomplishing your long-term goals. Humans are such a beautiful species because we have a strong desire to *learn*. We live, we learn, and we adapt by constantly acclimating ourselves to our environment based on what we've learned through experience. The action of learning, the desire to consistently improve, and the internal motivation to become the best version of yourself is what will launch you towards maximizing your potential.

Think of your learning process like a seed—a seed that you plant with hopes of becoming a beautiful, prosperous tree. Learning with the purpose of trying to be your best is a process much like that of the growing of a tree. I don't know about you, but I've never seen a tree blossom overnight.

Picture in your mind the largest, most splendid peach tree you can imagine. It takes years and years of following a process for it to reach great heights and bear wonderful fruits. That kind of growth is only made possible if the caregiver takes the small, consistent steps required to grow a peach tree, every single day. You plant the seed, find the proper soil, water it, make sure you give it enough sun and *bam*! Day after day, you've committed to a process that will bring you a profound peach tree. And because you made the decision to follow through on your promise, the potential of your peach tree has hit the summits! The process of learning follows a similar progression.

> **"The best time to plant a tree was 20 years ago.
> The second-best time is now."** —Chinese Proverb

Everything I've learned to incorporate into my daily routine has come as a result of reading books, listening to podcasts, and personal trials. My habits and actions are a direct result of my studies and aspiration to improve. Consistently trying to learn from the best, while always striving to be the best version of myself, has provided me with a chance at creating the lifestyle that I now call, "BTB."

Understanding how to gather relevant information is a massive component to BTB. That in itself, is how we *learn from the best*. I'm going to highlight what the process of learning from the best looks like and how you can adapt your mindset to become someone who loves to constantly improve.

Getting yourself in the right frame of mind is arguably the most important step towards your goal. Having the right mindset is like having the proper equipment before stepping out onto the playing field. Making sure you are well equipped to handle the pressure that comes along with stepping into the arena is mandatory. Prepare yourself accordingly by learning from the best.

This is the first step of your journey, so congratulations! By opening this book and reading up until this point, you've already taken it further than most. But we have a long way to go. Lao Tzu says that the journey of 1,000 miles begins with a single step. Let's take that step together. I want to provide you with the tools and inspiration you need to transform your life in an empowering way.

THE POWER OF LEARNING

What does it actually mean to learn?
How do I commit to becoming a better learner?

Unfortunately, many individuals link these phrases directly to the classroom or with school, as if that is the only place where one can learn. Because learning is linked with school and studying, we oftentimes automatically think that learning is *boring*. What a shame!

However, that is going to change now. Let me define learning for you, according to the dictionary. Learning is, *"the acquisition of knowledge or skills through experience, study, or by being taught."*

Beautiful. Simple. Powerful.

Every day we are put in situations in which we have the opportunity to discover how to improve our performance, be healthier, start a business, or make more money. All of this requires learning. Experts are not born as experts. They committed to actively learning everything they could about their field to become a master. In order to become someone who loves to learn, you must adjust your beliefs about learning. Transform your mindset and identify as someone who loves to learn, someone who is constantly trying to improve, and someone who is continuously striving to focus on your craft. Repeat these phrases to yourself in order to convince yourself and persuade your mind that you are a learner.

- "Leaning will help me succeed."
- "I am someone who is always looking to learn."
- "I am open to learning new ideas."
- "I enjoy learning new things."

Tell yourself you already are what you're trying to become. The potential power lies in your perception of your identity. When you tell yourself that you already ARE your goal, you will make decisions that support it. For example, how can you expect to quit smoking if you identify yourself as a smoker? If you identify as a smoker, you are going to do what smokers do. Regularly. You need to change your beliefs and reframe how you identify yourself. Try to adapt this point of view as you go throughout your days and try to look at everything you come across as an opportunity to learn.

If you identify as a learner now, think about what learners do daily, and how they live their lives. If you identify as an elite athlete, start making decisions that elite athletes make.

THE BEST TEACHER

We need to comprehend a simple truth that learning takes place 24/7. All around the clock, we are always learning on the go as we encounter new situations in our day-to-day lives.

Think of learning like storing documents in a file cabinet. As you continue to go about your day, have new experiences, and learn new things, your brain will be inserting your experiences into your file cabinet of reference for future use. I truly believe, deep down to the core, that the most influential way to learn anything in life is through your own *mistakes* and *experiences*!

Mistakes are *the best teachers*. What's tragic is that the average person views mistakes in the same way they do failure. Most of us think mistakes are something to avoid because they cause pain. I'm going to tell you right now to *ditch that idea*. Remove it completely and erase it entirely from your mind. Mistakes are the most vital part in the process of learning. They are the key to unlocking the door to your potential. Yes, they cause pain, but no pain no gain baby. We all know that line.

It's like working out. You work out, it hurts like hell, you're sore the next day, but hey, you're getting stronger! That's how mistakes work. Mistakes are like "working out" your wisdom. You try something, you fail, it hurts, but the reward at the end is more wisdom. This, my friend, is the only way to truly thrive.

> ## "Mistakes are the price you pay
> ## for the admission of improvement."
> —John C. Maxwell

Now, I'm not telling you to go into your job and purposely make mistakes just for the sake of making them. However, if you aren't taking any risks in fear of making mistakes, then that's a good sign you aren't challenging yourself enough and probably aren't growing. So don't be afraid of mistakes. Accept them and view them as a message that you're pushing yourself and that you're continuing to learn new things that will in turn, make you better. You have to make mistakes in order to learn from them. That is how you improve. That is how you make strides in every aspect of your life.

"Success in life is the result of good judgment. Good judgment is usually the result of experience. Experience is usually the result of bad judgment." —Tony Robbins

You're going to learn a tremendous amount along the way as different events occur throughout your life. Do you really think it's realistic to go through the crazy ride that life has to offer and never make a mistake? You would be setting yourself up for failure by striving for perfection. Manage your expectations and realize that screwing up is part of the process. Mistakes will happen as you find yourself among trials.

As you encounter difficult situations and are forced to make tough decisions, the concept of our *best teacher* does have a contingency. This principle only holds true, if and only if, you learn from the mistake! As you may know, mistakes may cost you money or time so it's crucial not to make the same mistake twice. What good does it do to make a mistake but to not learn from it? You would be doing yourself a disservice.

Let's say, for instance, a young boy touches the stove and burns his hand. He has now learned that the stove may be hot. Now he knows for next time to not walk up to the stove and lay his hand on the same surface. He made a mistake by not checking if the stove was on in the first place. By not learning from that experience, he would only cause himself more potential pain down the road. It's a simple example, but it's effective in interpreting the manners in which we learn and adapt every day.

In a podcast by Sarah Blakely and Tony Robbins, Sarah, the CEO of Spanx, shares that growing up, every night at dinner, her father would ask her and her siblings, "so, what did you fail at today?" If they didn't have something, he would actually get upset with them! He literally engrained it in their brains that if you are not failing and making mistakes, then you simply are not pushing yourself enough.

As you gain the awareness and consciousness that lies behind the importance of *loving* mistakes, you will start to see them as *building blocks*. You will begin to view them in a more positive fashion. This understanding will drive you to try new things and leave yourself at risk of making a mistake. Then when something similar occurs in the future, you can apply your newly refined strategy to make sure you succeed!

LIVE. LEARN. APPLY.

Books and podcasts have allowed me to expand my mind in many ways. The vast majority of my knowledge about stuff like discipline, habits, beliefs, and the power of thoughts are a direct result of me taking that *first step* to actually opening up a book and reading about them.

For most of my life, I didn't identify as someone who enjoyed reading, studying, or had a desire to learn. However, over the years I've changed these beliefs and now identify myself as someone who *loves to learn*. Now, my beliefs are stronger than ever because I've committed myself for long enough to have seen first-hand how the results of my studies and reading of books have directly impacted my life. That goes for both on and off the soccer field.

Today, I take a lot of pride in the number of ways I find to learn and the degree to which I choose to educate myself. I'm constantly trying my best to progress, and persistently looking to gain specialized knowledge from the best. Always seeking to be *the best version of myself.*

After seeing how the practice of reading books and listening to podcasts had vastly improved the quality of my life, it's one of the first things I recommend for anyone looking to progress in some facet of their own lives. I'm regularly referring people to books I've read that align with assisting them in solving whatever kind of problems they come to me with.

- If you aren't sure about how to build boundaries in your relationships... there's a book about it.
- If you want to improve your self-talk and think more positively... there's a book about it.
- If you want to become a real estate agent and dominate the housing market... there's a book about that too!

Whatever advice you're looking for, you can find a book written by someone who is near the top of the game in the field you're seeking. There is an unimaginable variety of books out there that cross off nearly any topic you can think of. They are usually written by highly respected individuals in those pertaining areas. With all of this information out there and with all of the resources that we have today, there is no reason why you cannot defy the limits pressed on you by society. The only thing holding you back, in this time of infinite abundance, is your own level of awareness, your mindset, and your beliefs!

I can't even tell you the number of times that I have told the people I love or care about to pick up a book and to be intentional about reading it. I've seen how reading books has drastically affected my life and I truly want the same for everyone around me. Now, I can't control whether or not anyone actually reads one book or another. It's their choice whether they want to commit to working on themselves. I know that if they do choose to do so and are intentional about learning and applying the material, that the results would drastically change their lives.

Opening up your mind and making the decision to start your journey towards becoming your best self will become your greatest wealth.

**"Formal education will make you a living.
Self-education will make you a fortune."** —Jim Rohn

As I am now living out my dream of playing professional soccer, I've learned many valuable lessons along the way that have helped me get to where I am. My love for the game sparked a fire in my heart. It made me try and find ways to continuously learn about the game and improve myself as a player, even when I'm not at the training ground. For me, the learning process that I love comes through reading, writing, recovering, and watching film—and it's a method that aligns with my passion of football. However, it wasn't always that way.

Growing up as a kid, I couldn't tell you how many times I heard people say things like:

- "The only thing that will stop you from making it is yourself."
- "If you want to be a professional, you need to be stronger mentally!"
- "You need to get in control of your emotions."
- "Your attitude might end up holding you back."
- "You need to get your head in check if you want to play at the next level."

In the introduction, I shared with you the story of my first book. In that moment, holding *"Mind Gym,"* I finally understood that I had to get out of my own way. I had to get over the mental barriers that could possibly hold me back from reaching my goal.

Because of that first book, I've changed. I'm still a kid from the suburbs of Chicago. A kid with a dream. But because of *"Mind Gym"*, I've become addicted to reaching my fullest potential. Making that initial decision has shot me along this journey of trying to become my best self. I'm obsessed with the grind and the process required to get there. And I now want to help others, like you, reach your fullest potential as well.

"Ordinary people have big TVs. Extraordinary people have big libraries." —Robin Sharma

Following *"Mind Gym"*, the domino effect began. I immediately wondered what else I could learn and who else I could learn from. What other areas of my life did I want to improve? I now read over 30 books per year, and I've absorbed so much information and learned a ridiculous amount just by forming the habit of reading a little bit every single day.

I gained the awareness of being able to receive counsel from some of the top athletes, entrepreneurs, businessmen, and psychologists in the world, all at my fingertips! Taking advantage of what is available to you is an irreplaceable component to the BTB method: Learn from the best! All of their knowledge and information is available to you and I want to be someone who continues to pass that message along. Why not seek advice from someone who has reached the top of the game in their relative field?

Think about it. You and I have access to this kind of advice from those who are considered to be the best of the best! That information alone is something that is valuable. Something that can help you reproduce similar results in your own life if you dedicate yourself properly. And it's all available for the small price of a book (or a podcast, or a blog, etc.). Why aren't we using these resources more?

It doesn't matter what you do or what your occupation is. There are a countless number of resources available to you, filled with suggestions from those who have already achieved greatness in their relative field. Are you a young athlete who has dreams of making it to the NBA? Look to get advice from Michael Jordan, LeBron James, Kobe Bryant, Dwayne Wade, or Derrick Rose. The Tom Brady's of football, the Tony Robbins of psychology and personal growth, the Warren Buffets of investing in the stock market, the Grant Cardone's of creating everlasting wealth through real estate, the Gary Vees of branding and marketing, or the Ed Mylett's of podcasting and entrepreneurship. The list goes on and on and on. Their tips and guidance are all obtainable and it's up to you to find it and use it to your advantage. Because now you know... and you have *no excuse!*

"Never take advice from someone you wouldn't trade places with." —Kelly Clarkson

Who have you recently asked for advice from? Does that person live a life that you'd like to live yourself? Anyone who you admire, who has reached the top of their pertaining field, has the success that you want, or the relationships you long for, certainly has something valuable to say that can change the course of your life... *trust me.* I recommend you listen to their stories and take notes on the experiences and mistakes they made along their way to greatness. Hundreds, even thousands, of the greatest success stories we have ever known have either written books or have had books written about their experiences. They explain what they learned along their journey and what brought them success.

Make sure you are only looking for advice from individuals who are, or have been, at your desired destination. If you were to look at one person who had all the success you desired, lived the lifestyle that you wanted for yourself, represented the values that you feel are important, and they had a book about how they created that life, wouldn't you want to know how? By taking the first step and opening up a book, you can look directly at their roadmaps and receive their tips on how to give yourself the best chance at replicating results similar to theirs. When you add valuable tips to your life that have come directly from proven characters, you are bound to build up a fantastic portfolio of tactics. The beliefs you manifest and the attitudes you support will propel you closer to accomplishing your goals.

Keep in mind that these highly-driven individuals are no different than you and me; they were just able to figure out some things along the way that helped them improve the quality of their lives, and they *did* them. They found different principles, new habits, and more empowering routines that worked for them in achieving their dreams. They were able to recognize and learn from things through their experiences that maybe we haven't gone through yet.

Shortly after completing *"Mind Gym"*, I ended up picking up another book. My girlfriend, who is now my wife, Googled "top books on sports mentality" and gave me this gem for my birthday. It had a sleek black-and-red cover, and if you like to read as well, you know that new-book smell—fresh and crisp. The book was written by Michael Jordan's legendary trainer, Tim Grover, and was titled *"Relentless: Good to Great, Great to Unstoppable."*

After reading through that book, there was officially no turning back. I learned so many precious pieces of advice about how to separate yourself from your competition. Tim Grover talked about how the only limitations you have in life are the ones you put on yourself. About how in order to win big, you must believe in your abilities, persistently work on preparing yourself, and consistently sharpen your craft to ensure you're successful, even in the toughest of moments. He shared stories about how Michael Jordan was relentless in chasing down his goal of being the best basketball player of all time. He wanted to be an icon. Tim explained how Michael was able to keep his cool in high-pressure situations because he knew he had put in the time to properly ready himself. He did everything in his power to win every single time he stepped onto the court.

The words I read deeply resonated with me as they were leaving the page and connecting with my subconscious mind. I felt a growing obsession to go out and to get to work. I wanted to learn how to overcome my fears and control my emotions without letting them take control of me. After reading *"Relentless,"* I truly became obsessed with maximizing my potential and working relentlessly on my craft.

The value I gained from reading that book can't really be put into words. It's why I'm such a big believer in reading. *Because you don't have to know these highly successful people personally to learn from their particular experiences.* Reading about someone else's understandings, mistakes, and missteps along their way to success can save you a lot of time and a lot of pain. If you are shooting for a similar goal, odds are that you will face similar challenges along the way. Reading about someone else's triumphs during their pursuit of victory can provide you with consciousness and important awareness that you didn't have before.

YOUR ACTION ITEM: Think about some things you'd like to get better at this year. Write down five things you want to learn, and brainstorm how you can learn them. Write down book titles, expert's names, courses, etc.

1.

2.

3.

4.

5.

Stop depriving yourself of the information that is out there that can help you achieve the life you desire. Knowing that this information even exists in the first place is already putting you way ahead of the pack. Now take advantage of that awareness. Take the first step and start your journey of learning from the best.

PROTECT YOUR ENERGY

Learning from the best not only comes from reading books or listening to podcasts by people you've never met. It also comes from those who are actually around you.

"You are an average of the five people you spend the most time with." —Jim Rohn

Money. Friends. Fitness. Take a look at those three words carefully. Now, what do all of these assets have in common? Any guesses?

These are all things that you can make back if you lose them. The one asset that you cannot replace is *time*.

Time is so valuable. *It's irreplaceable*. Don't waste your time. Protect your energy.

More specifically, don't waste time around people who aren't driven in the same way that you are as you chase your dreams. I know I can't be the only one growing up who was constantly fed the message that you are who you hang out with. Therefore, if you choose to hang out with ambitious individuals, you'll become ambitious. Spend time around pessimistic people who complain and give you every reason as to why you can't succeed, and you'll probably end up doing just that. Don't hang out with people who aren't as ambitious or on the same mission as you because, again, *you are who you hang out with*!

Here's a concept that has proven itself time and time again. It's something I've learned from the best. Surrounding yourself with pessimistic people who constantly victimize themselves can be an absolute poison as you try to achieve your goals. In order to be your best, it's vital that you spend a majority of your time with those who operate similarly to you.

If you are spending most of your free time with people who have small goals for themselves, go in to work late, leave early after a mediocre day, don't embrace the grind, and live for Friday and Saturday nights, those affiliations probably aren't going to help you accomplish your long-term goals.

Don't get me wrong. I'm not saying that these are *bad* people by any means. And I'm not saying that they are *wrong* for choosing to do what they do. In fact, they may be completely content with their lives. They may feel complete fulfillment and be loaded with joy by engaging in whatever those activities may be. That is great for them. However, if you are trying to achieve something great, you must separate yourself from anyone who weighs you down or just isn't on the same mission as you. Take the words of Otto Berman... *"It's nothing personal, it's just business."*

Create boundaries in order to protect yourself, your goals, and your energy. Decide what you're willing to put up with and what you want for yourself. You must understand that the negative energy and pessimism that roots from people in your circle may just be the dynamite waiting to blow your vision to pieces.

Having adopted the mindset of being someone who constantly seeks to improve, I've noticed that as I've continued to grow in my own ways, that means I'm also growing apart from others. I've mentioned how vital it is to separate yourself from anyone or anything that holds you back. That forces you to be more cautious and selective about who you choose to spend time with. And if you've never thought about this before, my point may cross you wrong. But honestly, *that is my intention.*

"Entry into my circle is more selective than a Rhodes Scholar."
—Russ

I want you to think about this and become aware of who you're hanging around. Are those associations pushing you, inspiring you, and motivating you? Are the people you spend the most time with making you a better person? What's the topic of conversation going around the dinner table? Are you talking about goals, ideas, or new concepts that have helped increase the quality of your lives, or are you just gossiping about others and reminiscing about the party last weekend? Spending time with other goal-oriented individuals who are also taking massive action towards their dreams themselves, shoots that energy back to you and can motivate you to do the same things. If you're on the right track with who's a part of your circle, keep it going. But don't ever find yourself being the smartest or hardest working person in the room. If that is the case, you are in the wrong room.

YOUR ACTION ITEM: Write down three relationships you need to reevaluate:

1.

2.

3.

Just a reminder, don't be afraid to state which relationships you need to reevaluate. This doesn't mean you should cut this person out of your life and never speak to them again. It simply means you may need to set a boundary or limit for how much of that person you can consume on a regular basis. Especially if they are weighing you down from being your best self.

OVERCOMING THE ODDS

In the next chapter, we're going to talk about the need for having a vision for your life and mapping out how to get there. A big part of that falls back on the foundation of learning from the best.

As you begin to separate yourself from anything inhibiting your growth, you'll begin to change for the better. The tips you begin to implement can help you gain a foothold on your opposition. However, as you start to climb the ladder and see your successes unfolding, you're going to have to adapt to new environments as you level up. The higher you go, the better and better the competition around is too. You'll notice how everyone is pretty good at what they do.

I'll give you an example. I noticed this concept when I made the jump from the collegiate level to that of the professional. I quickly noticed how much better every player was. The standard was higher. Everyone had specific attributes and skill sets that allowed them to take their game to the next level and play professionally as well. The number of guys who got drafted was slim in comparison to the entire player pool across the nation. And the number of those who actually succeed at the professional level is even smaller than the ones who only make it there.

The odds are always going to be against you. That means you have to scan your surroundings and search for alternative ways to separate yourself from others at your same level. Each time you take a step up, you have to find new ways to elevate yourself in front of the guy next to you or you're going to be left behind.

It's like the cycle of life... there is always someone on your ass, hungry, who wants to take your spot. So, what makes you better than the competition? What makes you better than the next guy? When you reach the tier of the elite, which you will, you need to understand how the small, little, incremental, details become increasingly important! They are the distinguishing factor! Paying attention to the details become exceptionally critical.

> **"The difference between ordinary and extraordinary is just that little extra."** —Jimmy Johnson

Once your field narrows and you are competing amongst an evenly skilled group of individuals, you have to find ways to constantly make yourself better in order to stand out. To separate yourself, you need to look for the miniscule, superficially insignificant things, and ask yourself what you can do to get that extra advantage. That one thing might make all the difference! That one thing might land you that client, get your foot in the door, or get you onto the team.

I hope you understand now how important it is to make sure you're always looking to improve and *learn from the best*. Take note of the steps they took in order to separate themselves and take action. Do what is required to put yourself ahead of your competition. Make the jump.

'There is freedom waiting for you,
On the breezes of the sky,
And you ask, "what if I fall?"
Oh, but my darling, what if you fly?"

Deepak Chopra says in his book, *"The Seven Spiritual Laws of Success,"* that the future is created in the present. In the day-to-day moments we are living right now. Your future is dependent on what you do *today*. Don't wait! Start by learning from successful individuals, the ones who have the things you want and live the life you desire. Apply their teachings into your life.

This, my friends, is the first principle in living out the *BTB approach.*

As you continue to learn from the best and implement these principles into your daily life, you will see how your vision to achieve the things you want can serve as an invaluable tool. See yourself accomplishing everything you want in your future, with no limits, through your long-term vision. Seeing your vision. That's where we are going next.

2

SEE YOUR
VISION

Take a second to deeply reflect about the things you want to get out of your life. Close your eyes, breathe, and try to get in touch with your deepest desires and aspirations. What do you *see*? What do you feel? What is your initial thought? What comes to mind? What is the vision you see for your future? What would you like to accomplish?

Why am I asking all of these questions? Because clarifying what it is that you want for yourself and identifying your goals at the beginning of your journey are fundamental to long-term success. We live in a world where you can do or be anything you want.

In order to map out your vision effectively, your end goal has to be something you are passionate about. If it's not, you won't find yourself taking the action required to make your vision a reality. Ask yourself this: Are your goals big enough to motivate you enough to take the actions required to bring them to life? Because in order to succeed against all odds, it's going to take a lot of work! If that work isn't aligned with something that you're truly passionate about, you're going to struggle to find the motivation and inspiration that will fuel you through the difficult times along your journey to success.

If you're chasing a paycheck, stuck working a job that you hate with co-workers you don't like, or feeling unfulfilled and longing for purpose; what's stopping you from quitting today and taking the first step towards building the life of your dreams? Yeah, you may need the income to pay your bills. I get that. You may not be able to afford to just up and quit at this given moment. But has it ever crossed your mind that you could be doing work that fulfills you every day if you're able to clearly identify what it is that you want?

CREATE THE MAP

If you don't start by seeing your vision clearly, you're not going to be equipped to create the map that will get you to your desired destination. If you were to get in your car with a desire to go somewhere you have never been before, what is the first thing you would do? Would you just pull out of the driveway and go for it? Probably not! You'd punch it into the GPS, of course! That way, you'd know where to go, where you'd have to turn, and what you'd have to do to get there. Even if there was construction along the way or an accident that required a detour, your goal of ultimately getting to your desired destination remains the same.

Now, let's take a second and use this example to envision another helpful picture. We will have two hypothetical situations.

Situation 1: The destination is somewhere you don't really care about going, somewhere you feel indifferent and unexcited about visiting.

Situation 2: The destination is your dream location. Somewhere you've been dying to visit since you were a little kid. Somewhere magical. The idea of visiting this place brings you pure joy and makes you feel extreme excitement.

Now, think about how much the destination plays a role in your levels of motivation. What if something were to come up along your journey that required you to find a different route—a storm, an accident, a roadblock, etc. That new route might just add a few more hours to your trip, and it could make the journey ten times worse, longer, or harder. What would you do? In situation 1, even if the change in route is minor, you might just turn the car around and go back home. Why? Because your desire and hunger to get to that destination isn't strong enough! You would be less inclined to try and find another way. It would be easier to quit, to say that it just wasn't meant to be, and to forfeit the possibility of arriving at that desired destination. But, if you came to a block in the road in situation 2, where the desired destination was somewhere you were dying to go, you would *find a way*! No matter how long it took, no matter who or what was standing in the way, and no matter how many times you had to reroute, you would find the motivation and inspiration within yourself to see out the journey. You would much more likely make the sacrifices needed to succeed and reach your destination in situation 2 than in situation 1.

Your vision must align with something that will make you feel fulfilled to the highest degree. Your vision should align with your passion and push you to get out of bed every single day. It should fuel and inspire you to get to work, to try your best in building the life of your dreams. If your vision isn't connected to something that you're deeply passionate about, you won't find yourself taking all of the necessary steps in order to become who you want to be.

We see it far too often where individuals are trapped doing something that they aren't passionate about, in a line of work that doesn't fulfill them. Unfortunately, they don't see a way out. There's no light at the end of the tunnel. They don't have the courage to step up and drive change. Too many are comfortable and content with just getting by and making enough to pay their bills.

For those of you that want to exceed mediocrity, the first step is to strategize a way out. I'm not denying the fact that it's scary and requires risk. Doing so requires bravery, commitment, and a ton of self-belief. But don't let the possibility of failing stop you from acting. This life is full of unlimited abundance and there is enough out there for all of us. Life's greatest rewards are being saved for those who are willing to act and chase their dreams in spite of the presence of their fears. See and identify your vision *clearly*, then take action towards creating it.

> ## "People overestimate what they can do in a year, but underestimate what they can do in 10." —Bill Gates

YOUR ACTION ITEM: What's your desired destination? In as much detail as possible, write down your vision in the space below:

HIGHS AND LOWS

Imagine yourself in five to ten years and envision the emotion of what it would feel like to *win*. To achieve whatever it is that you've been working so hard for. Imagine how it would feel and then remember that feeling. That envisioned feeling is key to providing you with the extra source of fuel to keep you moving forward when things don't go as expected.

Life doesn't always go "according to plan." Some days may be good while others may be more challenging. Think about it. If you and I only worked towards our goals on the good days when things were going great, we wouldn't get very far, now would we? It would be impossible to stay consistent in your daily routine and habits if you only acted when you *felt* like it. Almost anyone can stick to their routine when everything is going their way. If everybody was always "in the mood" to do the things the things they needed to do, then we'd all be living out our dreams, wouldn't we? Life would be great if that was always the case. Everyone would be successful. Safe to say that it's much easier to be disciplined in your habits and willing to strive towards being your best when you're feeling up for it.

Here are some scenarios that display what I'm referring to when I say that "life is going your way:"

- The days when you wake up feeling energized after having a good night's rest.
- The days when you close the sale that you've been working so hard for.
- The days when you wake up feeling rejuvenated because of the promotion you just received.
- The days after you scored the game-winning goal.

Sounds great, doesn't it? These are the days when you can tell yourself that you're doing the best you can with ease. When striving to BTB seems like no problem at all. These are the times where your input is beginning to provide the output you desire. When the things you're doing every day seem to be working. The days where you start to see some major payoffs for all the work you've been doing. *You feel on top of the world.*

It's simple to see your vision clearly during those times. You will find confidence in knowing that everything you've ever wanted is going to come to fruition in the future. These are the days when the extra work that's piled up on your desk seems a bit more appetizing. Doing a little extra feels a bit more necessary because you're in a good mood and you feel like doing it. How good does it feel when you're able to tick off all of the habits on your habit tracker as you are trying to build momentum throughout your days and weeks?

During the MLS Combine, I had the privilege of meeting the late legendary coach Sigi Schmid. One of the most decorated managers the MLS has ever seen. During my interview with the LA Galaxy, he gave me a piece of advice that I carry with me to this day. At the end of my interview, I had prepared a question beforehand to try and make sure I took something away of true value. I asked him, "what advice would you give a player in my shoes, who is heading into the MLS as a rookie? Because I've seen so many guys make it to the league, only to be gone after a year. What separates those who succeed from those who don't? What's the difference between those who play for years and have great careers, and those who don't?" He said, "the best advice I can give you as a pro is to not let your highs get too high or your lows get too low. Stay on a consistent path, up."

So, I left the meeting asking myself this question: How can I keep myself on a consistent path up, regardless of the highs and lows that I'm bound to face in my career? My answer was to remain focused on the long-term goals I set out to accomplish. To keep my eyes locked on *my vision,* for what could be.

Whatever it is you do, you're bound to face what Sigi referred to as the highs and lows. There will be days that are great. But unfortunately, life doesn't always work that way. As nice as it is to experience those feelings of certainty during the high moments, to have that strong sense of self-belief and faith in what you're doing, we also need to take a look at the bigger picture. So, let's get real. That fantasy ends here.

Let's take a step back and work on preparing you for when things aren't going your way. For when the opposite occurs. What some may call *reality*.

What happens when you are hit with a situation at work that pushes negative and disempowering emotions into the front of your mind? The days when you wake up in the morning and are groggy, tired, or not feeling well? The times when your competition beat you out and just received the promotion that you've been working your ass off for? What about when you don't get that spot on the team you thought you would? When your team loses the biggest game of the season and the opportunity that once seemed so grand all of a sudden diminishes before your very eyes? These are the times when building and seeing that long-term vision, *your vision,* will push you through to the end.

You need to be able to see beyond today and beyond your current circumstances if you want to achieve and succeed. Life is going to push you around, smack you across the face, and punch you square in the nose. You're going to fall and you're going to make mistakes along the way. Now is the time to make a conscious choice not to let the external situations affect your internal motivation.

"Nothing external can phase the internal." —Connor McGregor

The choice is yours. It's up to you whether you decide to rise above that adversity and fight the long fight, or not. The only other choice you have, would be to fall short and to victimize yourself. To feel sorry for yourself and to make up excuses as to why you didn't accomplish your goals.

Looking at yourself in the mirror and taking full accountability is no easy feat. That's a hard thing to do, especially when you're not happy with where you're at in life. But the wonderful thing about taking that accountability, that you are where you are because of what *you* did and not because of anything outside of your own choices, is that it gives you tremendous power. That power provides you with the awareness that *you* have the capability to change the trajectory of your life. It's your internal motivation, your actions or inactions, and your choices that will shape the outcome of your future.

Having an empowering vision and making your long-term goals clear are *the* foundation to success. If you were to draw up a blueprint and start building a house, you wouldn't start by laying down twigs, leaves, and small rocks, now, would you? Your house would easily be blown away by a storm. What you would need is concrete. Something rock solid, tough, and durable. A sustaining foundation because, like I mentioned above, things aren't always going to go your way!

The weather isn't always going to be sunshine and rainbows. The wind is going to pick up, it's going to hail, rain, lightning, and thunderstorm at some point in your life. Doubt is going to creep into the back of your mind when something doesn't go according to plan. When you start to doubt you can do it, when others criticize you, or when outsiders call you crazy. In these times of trial, the foundation of your vision will hold strong! Your vision and your unwavering belief that no matter the bumps in the road, no matter what life throws at you, or what obstacles you may stumble across, *you will succeed*!

> ## "Change your approach as necessary, but never abandon your ultimate vision!" —Tony Robbins

Tony's words are incredibly valuable and relevant to the point. How you get to where you want to go might need adaptation and require you to be flexible in your approach. However, once you've decided what you want for yourself, you must never let go of that vision—your final product and your end point. Slight modifications in your approach may be necessary, but don't ever lose sight of where you ultimately want to go! Your long-term vision and your belief should go far beyond the minor setbacks that you might face today or tomorrow.

Familiarize yourself and adapt to your environment. Improvise on the go. Do whatever it takes to get through the ups and downs in order to bring your vision to a reality. The sparked ignition that comes through seeing your long-term vision, all while you're learning from the best, is the X factor in reaching your desired level of achievement. Build that unwavering belief and know with certainty you will receive what you want over the long haul. That my friends, will give you the extra gas you need to drive through the extra mile.

VISUALIZING

A few years back I read a book called *"The Inner Game of Tennis."* The author, W. Timothy Gallwey, provides numerous examples as to how powerful the human brain can be in determining what we want. Gallwey describes how your brain cannot tell the difference between a vivid, in depth, detailed thought, and actual reality. The chemical reaction that starts to happen in your brain and body if you were to imagine yourself hitting a tennis ball with perfect technique, would be nearly identical to the reaction that would take place if you were to *actually do it*.

"Whatever your mind can conceive and believe, you can achieve."
—Napoleon Hill

I heard another example of this technique listening to the Ed Mylett show while stuck in traffic on the way home from practice one day. This specific episode caught my attention, I remember, because of its title: *"Visualize Your Victory."* The guest on that show was one of the best golfers of all time, Phil Mickelson. During the podcast, Phil explained the power of visualizing and seeing shots in your mind before stepping up to the ball. He referred to a study conducted years ago that examined the effect that visualization practices could have on three groups of basketball players, all looking to improve their free throws. One group only practiced their free throws physically, another practiced both physically and mentally by visualizing, and the last group was to practice their free throw shooting *only* by visualizing.

Phil described how the results forever changed his pre-shot and practice routines. The biggest difference between the groups came from the group who only practiced physically. The other two, that both practiced visualizations, saw staggering improvements in their free throw shooting ability. Moral of the story? Visualizing is a powerful tool, and one that we have at our disposal 24/7.

The human brain is a mighty device that we should learn how to use to our advantage! If you can thoroughly envision yourself engaging with the actions you desire, your brain will not be able make the distinction between real experience and your imagination. When you are able to harness this formidable source of energy, you will find yourself feeling an enhanced sense of accomplishment as to what is possible for you in your life.

The influence of visualizing yourself and seeing yourself succeed has proven itself worthy time and time again. People all over the world who have achieved ridiculous levels of success, swear by it as well. In the book I mentioned earlier, "*Mind Gym*," I remember Gary Mack going through a pregame technique used by one of the greatest soccer players of all time, Pele! His methodology for getting ready for a game was unlike most other players on his team, and better yet, most other players in the world. Instead of following the crowd and warming up with stretching, riding the stationary bike, or some other kind of physical prep-work, the majority of Pele's preparation was mental.

He would find a quiet place in the locker room where he could be alone with his thoughts. He'd grab two towels, one for underneath his head and the other to cover his eyes. Then he began to replay some of his best moments on a highlight reel in his mind. The tape he visualized included some of the best goals he'd ever scored and some of his greatest moments throughout his career. Winning trophies, beating the defense, embracing the true feeling of success, and seeing himself dominate the game. Physiologically, his state would immediately change after watching himself score and win, over and over again. His confidence, therefore, was blaring through the roof before the match, and the warm-up hadn't even started! After visualizing and seeing himself succeed on numerous occasions, Pele's mind was primed, and he was ready to go when the whistle blew. As confident as ever, Pele' would play the game with absolute certainty that he was the best.

Pele's consistent practice of mentally preparing assisted him in scoring over 1,000 goals throughout his career. No one could stop him after he harnessed the power of seeing his vision and watching himself succeed time and time again.

Like with Pele', visualizing your desired destination and the success you wish for, can kickstart the process of making it a reality. The vision you have for yourself, in collaboration with the power of the human brain, can be *the* difference in helping you achieve your goals.

YOUR ACTION ITEM: Lay down in a quiet place and set a timer for 10 minutes. For 10 minutes, with no interruption, just lay there and visualize yourself succeeding at your goal. Try to incorporate all 5 senses. Focus on what it feels like, sounds like, tastes like, smells like and looks like. If your mind drifts, that's okay. Just guide it back. Visualize for 10 full minutes. Try to do this every single day and watch how it impacts your life.

SEEING PAST YOUR FAILURES

No one ever became successful or achieved greatness from sitting back, waiting, and hoping for something miraculous to happen in their lives. Victory and the glory that comes with it doesn't just fall out of the sky. The time is *now* to stop wishing for your lottery ticket and to stop expecting to get rich quick. Find the courage to be bold and act in spite of your fears. Come to grip with the fact that you might fail; accept the reality that you may not succeed the first time around. Fortune always favors the bold!

"Insanity is doing the same thing over and over and expecting different results." —Albert Einstein

At the end of the day—whether it's your first idea, your first business endeavor, or your first time trying to run a company—things might not work out exactly like you planned, and that's okay. The real success comes to those who just do, and don't just wait.

Let's create a hypothetical situation. What if you had been trying to accomplish a goal that you had failed at two, three, four, or even five times? Would you draw a line through it and cross it out because it initially didn't work out? That's a question you need to ask yourself.

I was listening to *"The 5 Second Rule,"* by Mel Robbins, on audible recently and she mentioned something that utterly blew my mind. Are you familiar with Dyson vacuums, one of the best cleaning machines on the market today? Well, let me tell you something that will knock your socks off. The man who created the Dyson vacuums had made over *5,000 prototypes* before creating the one he felt was suitable and equipped to do the job of cleaning your floors! You read that right. FIVE THOUSAND!!!

James Dyson himself states, "I made 5,127 prototypes of my vacuum before I got it right. There were 5,126 failures. But I learned from each one. That's how I came up with a solution."

"There is only one thing that makes a dream impossible to achieve: The fear of failure." —Paulo Coelho

You'd think at some point it might have been easier for him to just throw in the towel, no? Seems like it would be hard to keep going, doesn't it? The easy thing to do would be to quit, because hell... you've tried and tried, over and over again, and nothing seems to be working. But that's why we know his product today... all because he had *the relentless desire* to achieve what he longed for, his *vision* of what could be. He had a dream of what the perfect vacuum cleaner could be and saw that vision with true clarity. He brought his idea to reality because of his persistence and determination to push past each failure. He saw each and every misstep as a stepping-stone. The most successful people are able to maintain their long-term vision and belief regardless of their temporary disappointments. Simply because they don't focus on the severity of their setbacks. They learn and continue to move forward!

Now, let's go back to the situation where you've "failed" a few times during the beginning stages of your journey. You've tried over and over again, making constant adjustments and little tweaks trying to figure out the issue, and you've repeated this process over five times. Now, think about this... What if your breakthrough was waiting for you the sixth time? If you gave up at one of the steps from one to five, you would never know what was waiting for you on the other side of the door of persistence. Before you start your quest to be the best, *see your vision!*

SPEAK YOUR VISION INTO EXISTENCE

A methodology I truly believe in is speaking your visions into existence. Speak them into existence with your close friends and family and experience the emotions together of what it would feel like to get the things you utterly desire.

When you go out with friends or family, what are the topics of conversation? Have you ever noticed how after talking about the most recent breaking news, the latest catastrophes, or engaging in gossip, that those discussions drain your emotional well-being? I can't stand it. I really try to make sure I am aware of what I am talking about with my closest friends and am extra cautious when it comes to our topics of conversation. I feel a much more positive energy flow through my body when my friends or my family and I talk about our personal goals, our ambitions, or just some positive food for thought.

I couldn't even tell you about the number of conversations that I've had with my inner circle—my people—about what it will soon feel like to accomplish our dreams. Imagining reaching the top of the mountain and thinking about how much different life will be, and how fun it will be to look back on those times when we used to talk about the things that we are fortunate enough to do now.

I'm a huge believer in the idea of speaking your dreams into existence because I truly feel like it helps you bring them to reality. The conversation itself completely wraps your mind around the idea and possibility. You almost feel like you already have it when you talk and act like you already do. These topics of conversation set you up for the life you are going to live. They allow you to imagine the unforeseeable and have an outstanding vision for yourself and for your future.

It's almost like making a promise to yourself. The importance of having big dreams that will inspire you to take a massive amount action is not up for debate if you want to achieve something great.

THE POWER OF VISION

Take a second right now to thoroughly imagine yourself reaping the rewards for all of the hard work that you put in every day. Once you step into that experience, you'll find yourself feeling more motivated than ever to take action right now towards building the future you want for yourself. When you learn from the best, when you can see your long-term, powerful vision, you're already taking the necessary steps to change your life for the better. I believe in you and support your vision for success. You can do it.

Chapters one and two are fundamental to BTB. They provide the framework and foundation for the beliefs and mind-set that is required to defy the odds and push pass the limits. Make sure you're always looking to learn from the best and that you never abandon your ultimate vision. The following chapters are going to provide you with tools and techniques on how to stay consistent in your routines and build a process that you can take in order to make your dreams real.

Coming up next is learning how we can continue to use the tools we have already assembled by applying what I call, "Three D's" to your everyday work.

Remember, develop a long-term vision, see it clearly, speak it into existence, and use that fire to power you through the ups and downs along the way.

"If people aren't laughing at your dreams, your dreams aren't big enough!" —Robin Sharma

Don't be afraid to dream big with your vision. All the doubters will come back around when your vision comes to fruition. Which at that point, your train will have already left the station. Your vision will act as the additional fuel to propel you towards your goals. Manifest them and take advantage of the power of your vision.

Let's continue to make strides! We're going to start paying massive attention to the details. *Applying the Three D's* is up next. Let's get it...

APPLY THE
THREE D'S

YOU VS. YOU

I n life, we all face challenges of our own when it comes to our day-to-day lives. Although not always big, we are constantly pressed by the little conflicts and mini battles that take place in our own minds. All day long, we fight the energy of resistance that is ultimately acting as the thief, robbing us from the joy that lies on the other side of taking action towards our goals.

The match that is continuously fought happens to be you vs. you. Your headspace is the battlefield where the fight between your conscious and subconscious mind never ends. It's that little voice in your head that speaks to you whenever you're about to make a decision or a choice. The voice that is constantly providing its input and dictating much of your everyday experiences. This advice that we give to ourselves can be helpful, but more often than not, it is detrimental. There are times when our conscious mind provides us with a list of excuses and/or reasons as to why we don't need to take action towards our goals right now. Here are some examples:

- You have time.
- You can do it tomorrow.
- You're tired.
- You don't really feel like it.

Often, we are lured away from accomplishing tasks that require deep focus. We are persuaded to instead engage in activities that are easier on our minds or that don't require as much thought as the things we know we really should to be doing. Stephen Covey, author of "*The 7 Habits of Highly Effective People,*" calls these "quadrant II activities." Examples of activities that fall into this category are our tasks that are not urgent, but important. Things like reading, journaling, meditating, exercising, or investing in our relationships all are quadrant II activities. We all know that these activities are important, however none of them happen to be urgent either. And because they aren't urgent, we often procrastinate their completion. Even though we sometimes persuade ourselves in the moment *not* to act and *not* to do what we know we need to be doing, our subconscious usually knows that, realistically, we should be knocking out the things on our to-do list.

"Procrastination is the fertilizer that makes difficulties grow." —John C. Maxwell

Is it just me, or do you find yourself fighting these same temptations and distractions? Do you have these same thoughts and arguments with yourself? Do you struggle to take action? Are you easily swayed by the distracting voice that is taking away your chances at creating success? I haven't lived a day of my life where I haven't experienced this kind of resistance! It's something universal that pulls at our attention, throws us off of our routines, and disrupts our consistency.

What do you find yourself struggling with most? For some people, they find it harder to gain clarity on what it is that they really want out of their lives. They're dying to know their true purpose and are relentlessly trying to find their passion. For others, they know exactly what it is that they want, but they struggle to find the commitment and consistency in their habits to do what is required to get it. There are also some people who don't know how to motivate themselves at all and struggle completely to get themselves out of bed every day. We are all human and we all face these kinds of adversities in our lives. The question is, are you going to let that pull, that resistance, win? Are you going to lose that battle that is *you vs. you* and fail to listen to your call to action?

To tackle those kinds of challenges, applying the *Three D's* will give you the upper hand. If you implement the principles aligned with the *Three D's*, you'll better your chances substantially at attaining glory. People who achieve great success have a burning *desire* to accomplish their goals, fine-tuned *discipline*, and uncompromising *dedication*.

DESIRE

The first of the three D's is *desire*. What does desire mean to you? According to the dictionary, desire is defined as, *"a strong feeling of wanting to have something or wishing for something to happen."*

> ## "Desires are seeds waiting for their season to sprout. From a single seed of desire, whole forests grow."
> —Deepak Chopra

Now we all know that wishing and wanting alone won't bring your visions to fruition. However, harnessing the power of *recognizing* your deepest desires, I believe, is essential to any amount of sustained success. Having desire can be understood as an internal motivation. Desire is having the willingness to do something, and actually follow through. To actually *do* rather than talk about *doing* speaks volumes, actions speak louder than words. Making the choice to follow your gut, to trust your instincts, and follow your desires, will greatly increase the likelihood of you accomplishing your goals. If you don't locate your deepest desire, there is no chance you'll be able to maintain your focus as you start to face challenges!

Think about it for a second. Be real with yourself. First, try to think about the things that you want. Second, think about *how badly* you want them. I encourage you to be open-minded, honest, and blunt as you evaluate what you believe your desires are. For me, at the end of the day, whether I do something or I don't, whether I follow through on something I said I would do and didn't, it all comes down to the brutally truthful question: *Do I want it bad enough?*

You may be thinking I'm being a bit harsh, but bear with me. Let's say that you are trying to lose some of the extra weight that you've been carrying around for the past couple of years. You've been trying to increase the number of times you work out and exercise per week, all while trying to eat a healthier diet and shifting to maintain a healthier lifestyle. However, you just can't seem to find yourself taking the necessary measures to accomplish the task. You can't find the courage to get yourself out of bed an hour earlier than you're used to in order to give yourself enough time to hit the gym. You can't seem to find the motivation to actually cook a couple more meals a week, rather than eating out on your way home from work. Now, why do you think that is—if *you are really being honest with yourself*? Take a look in the mirror and be completely straightforward. Don't cut yourself any slack. A big part of being successful in this area comes when you decide to hold yourself to a higher standard by *holding yourself accountable.*

David Goggins talks about how this concept of being brutally honest with himself changed his life. Holding himself to a higher standard than he ever had before. He started to stick little Post-It note messages on his bathroom mirror to help hold himself accountable. He would write down things he did during the previous day that he said he wasn't proud of. Having that reminder, a Post-It note stuck to the mirror for him to look at every day, forced him to confront himself and fix whatever it was that he had written down.

> **"When you look in the mirror, you see the only person you can't lie to."** —David Goggins

What would you have to say to yourself when looking into the account-ability mirror? Because, to a certain degree, the answer you're looking for might lead back to *desire*. In my opinion, it is very clear and simple. *You must not want whatever you say you want, bad enough*! You must not really have the *desire* to get healthier or to get in shape. If you know that exercising will help you lose weight, and that eating more nutritious foods will also assist you throughout the process, awareness isn't your problem. You must just not find it that important to eat better and exercise regularly. Otherwise, you would *do* it! Right? You would actually do what is required to get yourself to get into better shape if you *really* wanted it that bad! It really is that simple! Your *desire* doesn't run deep enough to motivate you enough to take the action that is necessary for you to reach your desired destination.

Let me propose to you a spark—the beginning of the solution to your struggles of acting in a way that doesn't align with your desires. The key element to understanding what drives us as human beings to take action is something that I learned from Tony Robbins. In one of his many books, *"Awaken the Giant Within"*, he talks about how every single one of our actions are driven by our needs to either *gain pleasure*, or *avoid pain*. That goes for everything you do. Every little decision and choice we make in our lives is linked to these two emotional contingencies. Remember this and inscribe it into the forefront of your mind. All of your actions are driven by your need to either gain pleasure or avoid pain.

Anyone can tell you until they're blue in the face the reasons why they think you don't take action. They can tell you that it's because you don't want it bad enough and that you don't desire the outcome enough... but let's be honest. What does that do? Does that really help the situation? No. Probably not. Because no one wants to hear that from anyone. Just telling you that you simply don't want to change bad enough isn't effective. That in itself isn't going to help you dig deeper into the root of the actual problem. That band-aid won't heal the wound and fix the pain that is disrupting your consistency beneath the surface. Your perceived pain is going to keep on creeping up and biting you in the ass as you continue to move down the road. We need to tackle the root of the problem. So, let's walk through a different method. I like to call this concept *linking*.

"Impossibility has no power in the face of genuine desire and uncompromising sincerity." —Kapil Gupta

FIND THE LINK

Have you ever thought about what you *link* your pain or pleasure to? I think a quick example would help clarify the concept of *linking* and how to do so effectively.

Let's go back to the individual looking to live a healthier lifestyle, trying to cut down that number they keep seeing pop up on the scale (an issue that many people face every day). Now take a look at this. Maybe they can't find the motivation to hit the gym and to eat healthier because they're *linking* going to the gym with their desire to get healthier.

- Losing weight and becoming healthier—*the apparent desire*
- Going to the gym and eating better foods—*the actions necessary to fulfill the desire*

The correlation might not be sustainable to fulfill such a demanding long-term commitment. However, have you noticed how so many of the stories about people who are able to make overnight life changes are able to do so after they've just flirted with death? They just had a heart attack, or a stroke, and woke up in the hospital on a ventilator and finally thought, "Wow, I really need to make a lifestyle change." They now have had an intense experience of pain so they're going to do everything in their power to avoid another experience like that. That sort of experience sparks lifestyle changes. If you were to *link* going to the gym with your *desire* to be alive in 10 years so that you're able to see your grandkids grow up, instead of linking going to the gym to your desire of to just "be healthier," that may be the push you need. That right there is a completely different level of *desire*. One that is strong enough to motivate you to take serious action. The desire you may feel to be alive long enough to see your children have children of their own, might be the reality check you needed that slaps you in the face.

Don't let yourself encounter one of these life-altering experiences, like a heart attack or a stroke, to wake up! Just as we learned how to use our vision to inspire us to take action, we can also use this practice in another way. By visualizing and feeling the pain *now* for what might happen *later* if we don't take action *today*. Evaluate what you're linking your desires to in your own life. Ask yourself if they're pushing you enough to take the action that would be needed in order to maximize your *fullest* potential.

Let's analyze the exercise of *linking* a bit further while placing the two motivating factors of avoiding pain and gaining pleasure in the front of our minds. One of the ways you can motivate yourself to take a substantial amount of action towards your goals is to do one of two things. First, you can link a massive amount of pleasure to whatever it is you want by truly seeing and feeling yourself accomplishing that goal, or you can do the opposite. Attach a substantial amount of pain to what it would feel like if you didn't/don't do what is needed to fulfill the dreams you're trying to make reality.

Linking helps create desire. When you have true *desire* to do something, you will find yourself doing whatever it takes to get the things that you want! I'm a true believer in this theory because I've seen how it has affected my personal day-to-day life, as well as noticing how it has vastly improved my consistency when I'm fighting the resistance to act.

Discovering your desires takes time to figure out. It requires deep reflection and self-awareness. But once you locate those truths—which only you can do because you're the only one who really knows—you'll be able to create a map. A GPS that will lead you and show you how to get to your desired destination. That happens by *learning from the best* and *seeing your vision* clearly. Only then can you link the emotions of pain and pleasure to your actions and habits. So, ask yourself these questions:

- Do you want to get healthier and exercise on a regular basis?
- Do you want to get that promotion that you have been working so hard for?
- Do you want to be able to provide yourself with financial security?
- Do you want to start your own business and be your own boss?
- Do you want to play professional sports and compete in stadiums in front of thousands of people?

Whatever it may be, find out what exactly it is that you desire and link a tremendous amount of pain *to not taking action* towards accomplishing it. It doesn't matter what your personal goal is. You may have answered "no" to all of the questions above because those aren't your desires. It will change on an individual basis.

As you take that massive step forward in locating your true *desire*, you need to strongly believe that you will reap the rewards for what you are sowing. Start by focusing on your goals, figuring out what steps are required to get yourself there, and then act! Draw yourself a road map by filling your heart, body, and mind with a vision that aligns with your *desires*.

You can't even start the process, though, if you aren't sure about what it is that you actually want. Trust your gut. Follow the sensation of your instincts. What are they telling you? Know that whatever it is you choose that you are going to chase it down with proper conviction. Commit to doing everything that is required to collide your desires with your reality.

YOUR ACTION ITEM. Right now, write down *your* desires. Take some time to really think about them. *Don't rush.* Put them on paper. What do you want to get out of your life? Success, happiness, certainty, significance, growth, or financial freedom? Think back to your *why* and engage in some self-reflection. Pinpoint desires that are strong enough to actually inspire you to take an insane amount of action. It's up to you to decide. Jot down a few desires below, and *be specific*:

1.

2.

3.

4.

5.

Now that you're on your way and can feel your desires with serious emotional intensity, they will motivate you to do things that you didn't find yourself doing before. That's because your *desires* align with your *passion*. Your hunger to achieve your end goal will be so strong that nothing will be able to throw you off track. The principle of linking your sincerest desires will pay dividends in the quality of your life when you utilize its effectiveness. Cultivate a state of mind where your desire to achieve your goals is so strong that they will push you through the ups and downs that life has to offer. Nothing can stop you except for the man in the mirror. You can always find a way!

"Crave the result so intensely that the work is irrelevant." —Tim Grover

DISCIPLINE

The second of the three D's is *discipline*. Discipline is a powerful word that can be defined in many ways because it means different things to different people. The dictionary chooses to define it as *"the control gained by enforcing obedience or order, orderly or prescribed conduct or pattern of behavior, or self-control."* In my eyes, discipline ties right into commitment and accountability.

- Commitment + Accountability = Discipline

Darren Hardy, author of another one of my favorite books, *"The Compound Effect"*, says that commitment is doing the thing you said you would do, long after the mood you said it in has left you. I can sit right here in my chair all I want and *say* that I'm going to wake up at 5 a.m. every morning right after watching a powerfully motivating video... that is, until my alarm goes off and I'm smacked in the face with the ultimatum of getting up and getting to work or hitting the snooze button and falling back to sleep. Discipline requires you to become the enforcer, the commander, and the general. You must realign your "cadet-self" anytime you step out of line! Remember to remind yourself constantly of your desires and fire up your levels of aspiration.

I cannot stress the importance enough of having a durable, robust, and solid foundation of *self-discipline.* You need to be disciplined, to an insane degree, in order to get yourself to your desired destination. Having versus not having discipline might be the most common fallout of those who never reach their full potential.

"Discipline is the bridge between goals and accomplishment." —Jim Rohn

One of the main reasons why having discipline is important is because of the fact that no one is going to fight for your dream harder than you! No one is going to wake up and put in the work on your behalf! If you want to do something that not many people have done, you're going to have to hold yourself to that high standard! That starts with discipline.

Discipline is the chief variance as to why only a few people, out of the billions on the planet, reach monumental heights. Discipline separates the best of the best from the rest of the pack. Most others cannot seem to figure out how these heights are reachable; they can't comprehend how these things that people are out here doing are even possible.

Being disciplined means being strong when others are weak and being able to see the big picture. That big picture is when the small, seemingly unimportant steps you're going through every day don't provide you with a desired short-term result. Being disciplined means being able to con- sistently push yourself through the difficulties, even though you haven't received that instant gratification that society has taught you to want so badly. Being disciplined to do something *every single day*, with a true belief that the steps you're taking will get you to where you want to go will be the determining factor for reaching new levels. Ones that you previously thought were unimaginable.

If you take a look at the most successful athletes, entrepreneurs, doctors, lawyers, businessmen, or CEOs, they all have an insurmountable amount of self-discipline and hold themselves accountable. I promise, this is a critical characteristic that all successful people have in common. They hold themselves to the highest standards. Every. Single. Day. They *do* the things that they have to do, even when they don't *want* to do them. You don't think everyone who is successful only takes action when they feel like it, do you? *Whether you feel like it or not doesn't matter*! How bad do you want to succeed?

Being great doesn't require only taking action every now and then to bridge the gap between you and those ahead of you. Taking these actions consistently enough to be able to see a difference down the road is what will create the life you desire. Alter your expectations and accept the fact that this process might take a while! And when I say a while, I'm talking about weeks, months, or even years. It takes time to do anything worthwhile. Accept that. Understand that. Believe that you are going to see the payoff from the investments that you put in on a day-to-day basis! Nothing worth having has ever come easy. If it did, everyone would do it.

Every one of my friends, family, and colleagues saw me on stage the day I was drafted into the pros., but they didn't see me during my college days where I would go for long runs in the blistering cold Wisconsin weather. They didn't see me in our training center after hours when I'd go in and work on my free kicks and left-footed finishing, or when I would stay in and watch film on a Friday night while everyone else was out at a party. No one forced me to do any of that stuff. No one was there to motivate or encourage me to do more even when I didn't really feel like it. That inspiration came from within myself because I believed that all of that work was going to pay off in the long run. Then, when I got drafted, it seemed like an overnight success to most other people. But the reality is that I'd been training, working, and preparing for the opportunity to play professional soccer every day of my entire life leading up to that moment!

What will someday seem like an overnight success, will really be the accumulation of small investments made over a long period of time. Your payoff will be seen when you find the discipline to do everything in your control to ensure your success. It's crucial to be disciplined enough to take those actions on a consistent basis, day in and day out. Why? Because people lose momentum when they don't see results as quickly as they'd like. People go to the gym a few times a week for a few weeks in a row and become discouraged because they haven't lost that much weight yet. That sense of defeat will usually stop them from continuing to engage in their healthy habits.

Be patient, be brave, and be persistent in your actions by focusing on winning each and every day. Building that momentum by being disciplined will allow you to separate yourself from the opposition. Finding ways to differentiate yourself, via resilient self-discipline, is a supreme competitive advantage. Engage yourself in separation season. Stay in your own lane. Limit your distractions. The interruptions that showcase themselves at one point or another will try to persuade you to make a bad decision. To miss a day. To break your cycle and lose track of the patterns you're building. Watch out for people or events that sway, confuse, and divert you off of the pathway you've created towards excellence. Whether that be a night out, binge watching TV shows, drugs, alcohol, social media... whatever it may be. Use that time, when others are engaging in those activities, as an *opportunity* to separate yourself from everyone else.

An opportunity? How can distractions serve as an opportunity? Because it's a chance for you to make a choice that will support your dreams. It's an opportunity for you to *separate yourself*. Stay in when everyone else is going out and get some extra work done! Trust me, I know this isn't easy. It's hard to become ultra-selective in engaging in fun activities with your friends all of a sudden because you've decided to chase greatness. I know it can be hard to say no sometimes, because a lot of us feel the need to fit in. We think it's in our best interest to just go along with the group, typically because we long to be liked by everyone or we don't want to miss out on something. That stops *now*. Today is the day you discover the power of self-discipline and muster up the courage to say no and to stay true to yourself and to your values.

Don't shy away from being different. Ultimately, saying no might be the most important investment you can make in yourself because you're showing that you believe in something bigger! The reason why I feel like I have a good handle on this concept is because I know from experience how when you have the strength to turn down the noise and tune out distraction, you can use that time to better yourself.

The first time is the hardest to say no because what you were once known for doing is not who you are anymore. Turning people down isn't easy, but once you adapt that identity and focus on the importance of self-investment, it will roll over and become a part of your character. Your bravery will accumulate and make it easier the next time for you to say, "no, I'm not going out tonight." When you do so, you'll feel even better about yourself, because you were able to walk away, block out those distractions, and you were able to stay focused on what you're trying to do. *All while staying true to who you really are. Your new identity of working towards the best version of yourself!*

As you continue the trend of being self-disciplined and making the right decisions, those actions will make a big difference as the number of times you decide to work on yourself add up. These are the moments you should relish the most. I know I do, and I know always will. I've reframed those circumstances when others are lured into distraction as, like I said earlier, massive opportunities. I view them as big-time chances for me to get ahead of the game. Whether that be staying in and watching some extra film, taking care of my body, recovering properly, or resting to make sure that I am prepared for my next training session—it all counts. Small decisions over time can make a vast difference in your future results.

Self-discipline is like a chain reaction. One action will lead to another and you will see the magic happen as you take steps in the right direction and are able to stay in your own lane. When the competition presses snooze, use those opportunities to get a head start. Give yourself all of these small advantages.

Having the discipline to hold yourself accountable is all you need. If you decide to give into the distractions and to continuously ignore your instincts, you will always miss out on these kind of opportunities. You will only be hurting yourself. If you don't have the discipline to follow through with what is required in order to fulfill your vision, you are doing yourself an injustice. You're only hurting yourself. Why? Because you're increasing the likelihood that you'll be living with the pain of regret in the future. Being disciplined in your diet, in your social life, and in your career are all necessary steps you need to take in order to reach your goal. You have to dig deep. You have to grind. You have to find that strong self-discipline within your heart. You have to hold yourself to the highest standards!

An exercise you can practice to help strengthen your self-discipline is to further your understanding between the difference of the *pain of discipline* versus *the pain of regret*. Think about it from this point of view... You don't want to look back on your life, say 10 years from now, and think to yourself:

- I wish I would have given a little bit more.
- I wish I would have done those extra reps.
- I wish I didn't go out as much.
- I wish I didn't care what people thought about me.
- I wish I would have worked a little bit harder.
- I wish I would have gotten up a little bit earlier every day.
- I wish I was more disciplined in my morning routine, diet, habits, etc.
- I wish I would have made a stronger commitment to my growth.
- I wish that I fell in love with the process.

This is where we can implement the strategies we learned in the *desire* section to link our emotions to push us to take action. These are the thoughts that you need to link so much pain to that they make you take the necessary steps that will support you making your dreams a reality.

When you have the discipline to follow your gut, to focus on your specialized knowledge, and to do your own thing, the payoff is so rewarding. It's an unbelievably remarkable feeling when you follow through and do what your instincts are telling you to do. When you act in a fashion that you know is right in the moment.

"We are all self-made, but only the successful will admit it." —Earle Nightingale

I saw this principle take work in my own life when I finally saw my first bits of success come around in my soccer career. After years of struggling, questioning, and stressing over what was to come, I learned the truth behind the universal law: you reap what you sow. I started to see for myself how you get out what you put in. That lesson came in the form of winning a Big Ten Championship, receiving multiple individual accolades, topped off by breaking a few national records, when I was a player at the University of Wisconsin-Madison. This accomplishment was so important for me because if I didn't have the Junior and Senior seasons that I had while I was at school, I wouldn't be where I am in my career today. I didn't have a big-time reputation where I would've been drafted regardless of my teams' success because of my name, or because I knew someone who could get me an opportunity, or because I was in the National Team pool as a youth player. By both the grace of God and relentless self-discipline, everything I have now and have received in the past has been *earned*. Nothing was given to me. I put in the work on my own and I wouldn't have it any other way.

To give you a little bit of background, my team was kind of the laughing-stock of the Big Ten when I showed up as a freshman. Sorry Badger fans, but it's true. Our first two years, we were at the bottom of the table and we had the furthest thing from a winning culture within our squad, let me tell ya! It sucked being one of the only programs on campus that wasn't successful. It seemed like every other team at our school was competing to be top dog of the conference. Our football, hockey, basketball, cross country, track and field, wrestling, and women's soccer teams were always fighting for national rankings and Big Ten titles. We had never even come close during my first two years. It was a dream that seemed so far-fetched at the time. It made me question what the differences were between teams and individuals who were succeeding in sports and those who weren't.

The answers I found were these. That it was only through a massive amount of self-discipline, a tireless work ethic, and relentless dedication, that I was able to hoist that trophy at the end of my senior season. I created life-changing moments and memories that I'll carry with me till the day God says my time is up. I'm extremely proud of that moment. It was a situation where I had given everything, my absolute all to accomplish that goal, and it actually paid off. The small steps that I was disciplined enough to take when others weren't, really worked out for me. That was only *my first taste* of what could be. What could I do if I was disciplined and dedicated in my pursuit to get the things that I desired? Because in this life, you get what you work for. It's one thing to set goals and dream about what could be. But to actually put an intense amount of work in to achieve your goals and prove it to yourself, that you can do whatever you put your mind to. There's no other feeling like it. Nothing compares.

Like anything else in life, the greater the reward, the higher the price tag. If you were to go to the store and buy the cheapest vacuum cleaner on the market, you aren't going to get the same quality as you would if you were to go all in and purchase a "top of the line" vacuum cleaner. The cheaper one is easiest to get, you don't have to spend much to take it home, but it will ultimately leave behind dust and lack the quality of the one that is known for being the best of the best. This analogy applies in the same way as your mission to achieve greatness. If you cut yourself short, if you go in cheap, you're going to get a cheap result. You need to be all in. You have to work harder to save more money to buy the best vacuum. You need to be disciplined in your routines and invest in yourself to ensure that your dreams don't leave behind dirt and undesired residue. It's as simple as that.

YOUR ACTION ITEM. In what areas of your life do you think you could be more disciplined? It's time to reveal the truth and be completely honest with yourself, once again. This exercise is meant to provide you with some self-awareness and redirect you towards creating the life that you want!

1.

2.

3.

4.

5.

I hope you understand how important it is to be disciplined. Hold yourself to the highest standards and don't ever settle for anything less than whatever it is you desire in your heart. Your desires can be manifested and brought to life in your material world if you're unremittingly disciplined. The better the prize, the higher the price tag. You are going to have to pay more if you are going to be granted access to life's ultimate gift, the one that is reserved for those who aren't afraid of saying no in order to *bet on themselves*.

DEDICATION

The third, and final D is *dedication. Committing yourself to a task or purpose.* When I hear the word dedication, I think about the process as a whole. The overlying summary of what the grind is and of what it takes to achieve true greatness—a dedication to yourself and to doing whatever it takes to reach your potential. True dedication is committing yourself, fully, to the aspiration of trying to become something greater than yourself. Through the ups, the downs, the late nights, the early mornings, the times where it's hard to get yourself going, when you're just not feeling up for it. If you aren't dedicated, if you aren't truthfully committed to doing whatever it takes, you will not follow through and complete your tasks. Fall in love with the process and identify yourself as someone who is dedicated. Embrace your dedication to your craft.

"The speed of your success is limited only by your dedication and what you're willing to sacrifice." —Nathan W. Morris

In my mind, someone who is dedicated *never* takes the time to contemplate how they feel before they act. You can't pick and choose between the things that you want to do versus the things that you don't want to do, because achieving greatness and overcoming tremendous adversity is going to require that you do things regardless of how you feel about them. Get over it! *Accept it.* There are going to be plenty of things that you're not going to want to do, but that's a part of it. To be truly dedicated means that you do what is necessary, no matter what mood you're in and no matter how you feel. The quality of your dedication, the degree to which you are dedicated, will provide you with direction. You won't always know what to do. But being dedicated will force you to learn as you go and to act on the move. Increase the dedication to your process and you will find yourself en-route to your desired destination. Only through dedication can you reach your goals.

Dedication combines all the aspects and components that we have talked about throughout this book so far. The constant, never-ending grind of striving to learn from the best. Consistently seeking and manifesting your vision, clarifying your desires and chasing them down with intensity. All capped off, by having the discipline required to follow through on the actions that will help you get what you want. *Dedication!* Anyone who has succeeded to a high degree in their field will repeatedly tell you that it took years of dedication to get to where they are today. To reap the rewards for what they were sowing. The process is, therefore, a dedication.

Think of your normal day. How can you enhance it? How can you be more efficient with your time? More productive? For your routine to be labeled as one that can be seen as a true grind. Think about your most produc-tive days. What do you usually do to make the most out of your time? Habitually, you would wake up before the sun has had a chance to rise in order to give yourself enough time to complete your morning routine. You mentally prepare yourself and armor your mind for the challenges you're going to have to face throughout your day.

You look at your daily schedule and you have meetings booked all day long at work. Assuming that you follow the standard 9 to 5 schedule, you then have to rush home from work, pick the kids up from school, put dinner on the table, and try to get your children in bed by a decent hour, and then what? Might it be time to get to work on your personal business? Maybe you put some time into your side hustle? Or is it time to invest and cultivate your relationship with your significant other? But that sounds like a long day! At least it does to me.

Your days may look a little different, but the important concept that I want to reiterate is that you're dedicated to one, building your dreams; two, investing in yourself; and three, enjoying the process by cultivating joy while doing it! When you finally get to bed and lay your head on the pillow, you'll be able to sleep *good*. You'll be able to reflect on what a productive day you've just had and fall asleep with a peace of mind! In my case, I find it easiest to get a good night's rest when I know I have shown relentless dedication towards my craft throughout the day. If I know in the back of my mind that I had not been productive, I might struggle to shut my mind off and rest properly. Have I done what I needed to do? Did I make myself 1% better than I was yesterday, as James Clear talks about in "*Atomic Habits*?" If I can answer those questions with a big fat "yes" then that is good enough for me. I rest assured, that I was dedicated that day.

It isn't always easy for me to follow through on the things I set out to do, though. I'm constantly fighting off that resistance as well. It's hard for everyone.

Let me give you an example of the resistance I'm talking about. So, a ritual that I have tried to incorporate into my daily routine has been to do 20 minutes of static stretching and 10 minutes of foam rolling, every day, before I get into bed for the night. I believe that over time, this will prolong my career by a couple of years and hopefully help prevent future possible injuries. That task alone takes 30 minutes. Doesn't seem like much right? Only 30 minutes a day? Others may think, "why bother?" In reality, what may seem like a small portion of your day—when you step back and take a look at the bigger picture —may be a crucial component to your long-term success. The actions that are *seemingly unimportant* are always the hardest ones to follow through on because it's so easy to trick yourself into thinking that you'll be fine either way. That voice of resistance arises and says, "I'll do it tomorrow." But, to have the discipline to follow through on those actions persistently, to dedicate myself to that process entirely, is the only way I would have any chance to see real results over time.

I've learned to *be dedicated* to lengthening and softening my muscles after tough days of physical training. I believe it will prove to be a habit that will be instrumental in accomplishing my long-term goals. Even though stretching is *not* an enjoyable activity for me, I find it in me to do it anyway. I never walk into my room and think... "Boy oh boy! Am I excited to stretch right now!" Nope. Never happens. But I don't even give myself the chance to contemplate. No asking myself if I feel like doing it or not. I've learned to just do it. As I've gotten older, its relevance has become imperative to my reliability on the pitch and a major aspect to maintaining top physical condition.

This is just a small example of how everyone can implement a new, seemingly unimportant activity into their daily routines. One that if done with true dedication, can vastly improve the quality of their life! Imagine what could be if you treated every endeavor in such a fashion. Where you committed yourself to be overly dedicated to it no matter what the action is. That, in itself, is how you form good habits, which ultimately shapes your circumstances and determines your destiny.

When you start to see the results that showcase themselves after being dedicated over a large interval of time, your actions add another penny into your piggy bank. That piggy bank represents the investment you make in yourself. These additions to your routines will further prove the point, most importantly to yourself, that when you dedicate yourself to consistent action, the payoff can be tremendous. Believe that everything you decide to do will make the difference for you when it's all said and done.

Whenever you find yourself coming across similar endeavors to the resistance you've learned to overcome or face comparable conflicts to the one's you've gone through in the past, you will have your experiences of triumph to look back on. Remind yourself that you can do whatever it takes, regardless of your circumstances. The knowledge in knowing that you can do whatever you set your mind to will give you all the reason to believe that you can accomplish yet another heavy feat. This is the process my friends. That is the grind. And when you act consistently over time, always with the intention of trying to be the best you can be, day in and day out, that by itself is a true dedication to the relentless pursuit of greatness.

> **"What we do on some great occasion will probably depend on what we already are; and what we are will be the result of previous years of self-discipline"** —Henry Liddon

Having the *desire* to do something, the *discipline* to be a man/woman of your word, and the *dedication* to follow through means you do whatever is required to make your dreams come true. Being dedicated to that process is how you build sustainable, healthy, and strong habits. Habits that can turn your life around completely and assist you in building the future that you want for yourself.

Too many people underestimate the power of habit. Building habits that will empower you and support you on your mission to become the best you can be, no matter how big or small, are the keys to unlocking the door of your potential. Habits will be discussed in the next phase of the journey. That is where we are going next...

ADOPT EMPOWERING HABITS

I want to kick off this chapter by providing you with one of my favorite quotes of all time. One that really opened my eyes to how powerful our daily actions can be in replicating positive results in our lives. John C. Maxwell, the author of over 30 high-quality books (ranging on topics of business, leadership, and personal growth), a frequent *New York Times* best-selling author, and a pastor/leadership/business expert, says this...

"You will never change your life until you change something you do daily. The secret to success is found in your daily routine."
—John C Maxwell

Changing what we do on a day-to-day basis is what ultimately will change the course of our lives. Therefore, we must adopt empowering habits and disengage from our disempowering ones.

What comes to mind when you think of the word "habit?" A habit is defined as *"a settled or regular tendency or practice, especially one that is hard to give up."* I feel like this definition insinuates that when someone brings up the conversation of habits, they're usually referring to the bad ones. We often link our habits to the negative actions that we find difficult to stop. Things like smoking, biting your nails, or getting emotionally triggered by something that's out of your control. But what about our good habits? The ones that positively affect our lives and increase our productivity? It's safe to say, no matter which way you approach it, our habits highly determine the quality of our days and the quality of our lives.

Habits are the actions we take throughout the day that we don't necessarily need to consciously think about. Think of the route you take when you drive to work in the morning. You know the route like the back of your hand at this point. You can drive to work while your mind is thinking about other, more important things because you have taken the same route so many times that you don't have to consciously think about it! You don't need to think about where to go because, subconsciously, you just know.

Habits aren't only actions we take, though. Habits can also be seen in the ways we think, the ways we react, the ways we perceive situations, and the list goes on and on. To sum it up, our quality of life takes a seat as the passenger while our habits take ahold of the wheel and direct our lives, regardless of where we want to go. Many people find themselves living their lives on autopilot, allowing their subconscious mind to dictate their actions. This usually tends to the bad habits that they've built over many, many years.

As you continue this mission to become the best version of yourself, I believe it's absolutely vital for you to understand how having good, positive, empowering habits can transform the trajectory of your life. Darren Hardy, NY times best-selling author of *"The Compound Effect,"* someone I refer to constantly, explains this:

"A daily routine built on good habits and discipline separates the most successful among us from everyone else."—Darren Hardy

How can we take this information and use it to our advantage? Well, start by analyzing your life by breaking it down from a day-by-day perspective. Before you can change anything, it would be helpful to become *aware* of the actions you are taking that may not be helping you achieve your long-term goals. A reason to be hopeful about building or removing a habit from your life is that it *can* be done with intentionality and purpose. You have the capability to change the direction of your life right now by altering and improving some of the actions you take daily.

> **"You can't change your destination overnight, but you can change your direction."** —Jim Rohn

One of the primary issues that most people face when trying to build a new habit starts with their paradigm. They can't comprehend how changing their actions every day, even if the changes are miniscule, can actually change their lives. The majority of people don't truly believe that if they were to do something consistently every day, even if the actions are small and seemingly inconsequential, it would actually make a difference anyways. So why try? What difference will it make?

A sizable portion of the problem lies behind the striking issue in many people looking for and expecting *instant gratification*. Everyone seems to be looking for a get rich overnight or a quick fix to their problems. Everybody wants to shine but nobody one wants to grind! No one wants to put in the work and get their hands dirty to create the results that they *say* they want. Most people are stuck, wishing that the pathway to their greatest potential and that the road to success didn't require any special effort or anything out of the ordinary.

The first step, if you are going to accomplish anything substantial in your lifetime, is to *alter your expectations*. Come to grasp this reality. Whatever it is that you're trying to do, it's going to require a few things that are non-negotiable:

- Awareness
- Intentionality
- Time

Success is waiting for you on the other side of a life built on productive, consistent, daily habits. You have to get the idea of it being easy and coming quickly, completely out of your head. You need to expect it to be a tough, long, and grueling process that is full of ups and downs. Unhappiness stems from your expectations being let down. So, if you can't change the fact that it's going to be hard and that it's going to take a long time, change the way you think about it. Expect the worst, pray for the best, and give it your all regardless.

One of the most rewarding feelings that you will feel in life is the sensation you get when you finally experience the payoff from something that you've truly earned and worked your ass off for. The feeling you experience when something is given to you doesn't compare to the feeling you will get when you choose to work hard to experience or acquire something that others haven't dared to do. When you grind and focus on engaging with empowering daily habits, it makes your victories that much sweeter, because you know that you've put in the work! By paying attention to the details and taking small, consistent steps over a substantial period of time, you will be given the opportunity to live a life of abundant success.

THE POWER OF COMPOUNDING

Commonly referred to as one of the most powerful tools known to man, the power of compounding has built quite the reputation for itself. Albert Einstein refers to compounding as the "eighth wonder of the world." Warren Buffet once said that he attributes all of his success to living in America, some lucky genes, and *compound interest.*

When you build captivating, consistent, efficient habits, you give yourself the chance to reap the rewards from one of life's most precious gifts. The gift of *compounding.* Take, for example, the compound interest of a penny that doubles every day. Have a look at the chart on the next page...

The Doubling Penny

DAY	VALUE	DAY	VALUE	DAY	VALUE
1	$0.01	11	$10.24	21	$10,485.76
2	$0.02	12	$20.48	22	$20,971.52
3	$0.04	13	$40.96	23	$41,943.04
4	$0.08	14	$81.92	24	$83,886.08
5	$0.16	15	$163.84	25	$167,772.16
6	$0.32	16	$327.68	26	$335,544.32
7	$0.64	17	$655.36	27	$671,088.64
8	$1.28	18	$1,310.72	28	**$1,342,177.28**
9	$2.56	19	$2,621.44	29	**$2,684,354.56**
10	$5.12	20	$5,242.88	30	**$5,368,709.12**

When you take a single penny and set it up to make specific gains over time, you can visually see how the power of compounding holds its own and can set yourself up for unbelievable long-term success. Notice, though, the total amount you gain doesn't increase much in the first few days or let alone even the first few weeks. You haven't even hit 100,000 on day 24! To see the results in your life or your business, you may not even see them for the first few years! The first couple of days don't show massive increases because we haven't given the compound effect a chance to make a true difference. You only start to see a noticeable incline as larger increments of time continue to pass by. With only 4 days to go in the month, from day 27 to day 30, you make a near $5,000,000 jump! The difference is made in the small consistent steps taken over a large period of time. When you create the habit of investing that penny and allow it to double for weeks, months, and years, that is when you will truly start to notice a remarkable distinction.

It's by the same method, just like the relationship between the doubling penny and compound interest, that your habits in your daily life work. They function in the same way. However, there are limitations and some challenges when speaking of habits that tend to showcase themselves more often than not. I see two in particular, that are revealed in the majority of cases as people try to build new habits. They are...

- Discouragement
- Missing or Skipping

The first of the two constraints come across as a form of *discouragement*. When people don't see results as quickly as they would like, they tend to stop acting all together. They get discouraged because they feel as if they have been doing a good job for a few days or weeks and assume that they should be seeing some results by now. Understanding the concrete truth of knowing that the process can take time is a virtue. Being patient, disciplined, and dedicated enough to consistently build and act on your habits is what will make the difference, even when you aren't seeing results just yet.

The hardest part is building the habit and engraving it into your subconscious; to the point where it becomes second nature. Whenever you're trying to make a major change to your lifestyle, that change is going to come as a shock to you because you're doing something that's completely out of the ordinary. If you're in the process of making a serious change, that is probably forcing you out of your comfort zone as well. You see it all the time. A number of different sources falsely indicate how long they believe it takes to build and engrain a new habit. I've heard 21 days, 30 days, 66 days, 90 days, but come on... who really knows? I think it's different per the individual. Once you decide to be intentionally consistent about implementing the new actions that you're trying to build in the form of habits, only then will they start to take shape in your life and become part of your daily routine. What once seemed so difficult will essentially take much less effort.

All change is difficult as I'm sure you know, but that goes for everyone and everything.

"Change is ugly in the beginning, messy in the middle, and beautiful in the end. Better daily awareness yields better daily choices which creates better daily results." —Robin Sharma

Yeah, it's going to be hard to make that initial change. Some days you might fail, but that's a part of it. Keep going, keep working and trying to be as consistent as you possibly can be. You will see the compound effect start to take place in due time. You will see major changes in all areas of your life as you reclaim empowering daily habits. *Identify yourself as a person who lives and dies by their habits.* Change something you do daily, and the world will be at your fingertips!

The second constraint is *skipping or missing* days along the way. The repetition of your desired habit is what will build and thicken the myelin in your brain. Daniel Coyle, in his book *"The Talent Code,"* explains how myelin is the insulation (made up of proteins and fatty acids) that wraps around the neural circuits in your brain. The more often you engage yourself in deep practice, mental struggle, and attention to detail, the thicker the myelin becomes. This process of creating more myelin is how you hardwire skills into your body and improve the neural pathway of electrical impulses from one neuron to another. Your practice of constant repetition will transform the unknown into the known so that your new habits are strong enough to have a place in your daily routine. You'll increase the literal energies in your brain by making mistakes, fixing those mistakes, and *repetition.* Find the book on the **BTB Website** at **www.bethebest-btb.com**!

The danger lies when skipping one day leads to two, and then three, and then four, and then a whole week goes by and you find yourself not having acted upon any of the habits you've been meaning to build on!

I cannot stress the importance enough of being *consistent* in your actions. This trait is absolutely mandatory if you are to see any sort of results. Pushing yourself to remain consistent is essential! It's what separates the professionals and the successful from the amateurs and mediocre. At the end of the day, if you're not able to repeat your desired actions, you won't create lasting results. And results are what everyone wants. Results are what all people are working towards. That sense of accomplishment.

As you gain the familiarity of triumph, slowly but surely, your next steps will seem much easier as you will have found the results you were looking for. Results give you proof that when you take consistent action with determination, discipline, and dedication, you can do whatever you put your mind to! This proof will be extremely valuable to you because a new belief will be formed. Your belief that after acting with strong repetition and by taking small, seemingly inconsequential steps, you are able to reach your goals.

However, as consistency is the most important aspect when trying to instill a new habit, it is also the most difficult to implement. It can be so easy to trick yourself into skipping a day or two when you think you have been doing good for the past three or four. It's a natural occurrence because people always think they deserve something. They feel entitled to a reward for taking positive actions.

The complacency of being satisfied with a few days or weeks of work will kill your long-term vision. You'll find people taking breaks in their routines as well, because majority of the time, those changes that we are trying to make are so small that if you were to skip just one or two days, *who would even notice*? No one. No one other than yourself. And the funny thing is, you aren't hurting anyone but yourself, either.

It's easy to brush your commitments under the rug and hit the pause button. It's easy to tell yourself that you'll get back after it tomorrow. That one lousy day isn't going to make a difference, right? Wrong. What's going to bring you to the next level is the relentless mentality in believing that one "lousy" day *will* make all the difference for you. That is what counts. It may not hurt you physically in that very moment to skip, but breaking the pattern of building a consistent habit can be detrimental to what you're trying to accomplish. One day can very easily lead to another, and then another, and then before you know it, you're still stuck in the same slump you started in.

Missing and skipping days will happen at one time or another. You most likely won't start off with a perfect track record. It's hard to create new habits and cut off old ones so don't stress yourself out to the point that you're causing yourself anxiety because of your desire to act. Just like with everything else in life, there is a balance to the construction of an empowering routine. So have some grace with yourself and work hard on being consistent. Do the best you can. If you end up falling off the horse for a day just hop back on and don't allow one day to turn into two.

You don't have any control over the past, so there is no point in magnifying your mistakes and making them bigger than they actually are. Just continue to learn, commit, and act. That's it.

YOUR ACTION ITEM. Positive or negative, the actions that we take every day, the things that we do all the time will be the number one determining factor in what shapes our destinies. We are in control. You can change now! The power to do so is within you somewhere. Find the sense and desire deep inside that is telling you to do something today. Right now! The beauty is in the moment and now is the time to grab ahold of your life and make some small incremental changes, some investments in yourself that will compound over time and change the direction of your life tremendously. Make an investment in your future by taking charge right this second! Write down five new habits you want to implement into your routine that you *know* will increase the chances of you living out your dream:

1.

2.

3.

4.

5.

I've found it extremely helpful to use a habit tracker as I go throughout my days, weeks, and months. This tool allows me to visually see my progress. This graph gives me the capability to analyze where I have done well along with my areas for improvement as the days and weeks go by. It makes adding new habits to your routine a bit easier because you're physically seeing the results, instead of just trying to remember them. Checking off the boxes also is psychologically satisfying, so it gives me the push and inspiration I need at times to continue to work. It pushes me to get another task done just so that I can experience the satisfaction of checking off another box! The habit tracker will help support you in taking that first step to changing your life because it will assist you in building new habits while breaking old ones. Most importantly a habit tracker helps hold yourself accountable along the way.

Get your Habit Tracker on the **BTB Website** for FREE at: **www.bethebest-btb.com**!

BECOMING A CREATURE OF HABIT

Over the years, leading into my professional career, I have grown into loving my identity as a creature of habit. I live and die by my routine and all of the little things I do every day to make myself the best I can be. I've become this way mainly because of the results that I've seen in the past coming from a direct result of the actions I was reproducing on a daily basis. The proof that I was talking about earlier, how my actions and habits led to a scenario where my vision came to fruition, and fulfilled itself. Since I fully committed myself to a process my junior year of college, the amount of growth I've seen occur in my life, from where I was to where I am today, is truly remarkable. And as the time passes by, my routine continues to change as I'm forced to adapt to wherever I'm at in life. But the *habits* I've built over the past few years haven't gone anywhere.

I'm not saying that what I do is right for everyone, that it's my way or no way, or that you should do the same. Not at all. I actually believe that every-one needs to find their balance as to what works best for them individually as I touched on earlier. I, myself, like to engage in deep work early in the morning. I believe it is the quietest, most tranquil time, and it provides me with a valuable hour or two where I can just think, work, and be with my own thoughts. Others may function better late in the deep hours of the night versus at the break of dawn. You need to find whatever works for you in your schedule and your lifestyle. As long as you're maximizing your time and running your days as efficiently and effectively as possible! However, if you were looking for a true test of discipline and mental toughness, waking up at 5 a.m. would certainly be a good place to start!

I would like to share a little bit about my daily routine to give you some food for thought to feed off of, and maybe to help lay a foundation of your own.

I've now become so engaged in my morning and daily routines that I have everything down to the hours and minutes. My alarm goes off at 5:00 a.m. every weekday. If I'm really tired, I might snooze it until 5:10, but no later than that! I like to wake up early because I had read in the past in Grant Cardone's book, *"10X,"* that 80% of millionaires are up before 6 a.m. In the book, Grant talks about how he's made it a goal of his, that no matter where he is in the world, he tries to wake up before the sun! That really resonated with me.

I also thoroughly enjoyed the messages and teachings I learned from reading *"The 5AM Club"* by Robin Sharma. I'm sure you've noticed because of how much I refer to its teachings! I made the choice after coming to a newly refined awareness, to apply those unique understandings as well. So once my alarm goes off, I count down from 5, to 4, to 3, to 2, to 1 and get myself out of bed. Once again, applying another technique I *learned from the best*, as a result of reading books. That technique is from Mel Robins in *"The 5 Second Rule."*

Once my inner clock strikes zero, I jump out of bed, no matter how tired I'm feeling at the moment. I don't contemplate or think twice about it. My daily routine has then begun and it's straight to the coffee maker. After pressing the wonderful button labeled "brew", I feed my dog and take him down for a walk. As I'm walking outside, embracing the stillness and serenity of the dark, peaceful morning, I'm still trying to wake up my body. As I walk, I intentionally try to inhale positive energy, feeling gratitude for waking up for another day and having the opportunity to continue to live out my dream! This process of brewing the coffee and walking the dog, I've learned, takes me around 15-20 minutes.

Once I make way back up the stairs, the coffee is ready, my cup has been poured, and I can begin my routine by starting off with my daily reading. I try and set a timer on my phone for 30 to 45 minutes so that I give my undivided attention to the material in the book. I don't let my attention wander until the timer goes off because, realistically, I have nowhere else to be and nothing else to do. I don't want to be tempted by any distractions, whether that's to look at my phone or be lured by some other less-important thought that doesn't have anything to do with the present moment.

After I read for that set amount of time, I'll set my book down and do 10 to 15 minutes of meditation. That varies between silent and guided meditation sessions. I like to change it up between the two because guided meditation, which can revolve around topics like confidence, gratitude, presence, or mental health, helps assist me in specific areas where I feel I may need some extra support.

Immediately after my meditation, I'll incorporate doing 10 minutes of visualization, where I visualize myself accomplishing my goals, playing with confidence on the field, and winning in all areas of my life. I learned this practice from golf legend, Phil Mickleson, where he talked about the importance of *"Visualizing Your Victory"* on the Ed Mylett show.

After seeing myself win, priming my mind, and putting myself into a positive state, I pull out my journal and write down three things I am grateful for *every day*. This practice of gratitude allows me to push all of these delightful feelings to the front of my mind, while also acknowledging my appreciation for everything I have in my life and all of the opportunities that have come my way. When I start my day by writing out and thinking of things that I'm grateful for, it also helps me to not dwell on things I may not have yet, or things I haven't been able to do at this point in my life. Again, anchoring myself on the present moment and being grateful for all of the little things that I do have! Writing these thoughts down helps me to stay in the now.

Once my meditation and gratitude exercises are done, I follow that up with some daily planning. Writing down what I have to do for the day and trying to create a schedule has been something I've found to be very beneficial. Once I've showered up and gotten ready, it's time to leave the house and head to the training facility. With some time on my hands before the training session, I can do my prehab (prep work before training) to make sure that I am feeling prepared, strong, and ready both physically and mentally before stepping out onto the pitch. Typically, we will be out on training pitch for right around 90 minutes, depending on the day of the week and how close we are to the game. The training time can vary based on whether or not I'm able to stay after and do some extra work to improve on a specific area of my game.

After training wraps up, I always make sure I will do some sort of cold, anti-inflammation recovery. Usually that's ice bath or cryotherapy. Once my post-training recovery—which includes gym work, rolling out, stretching, or riding the bike—is complete, I refuel my body with a nutritious meal and head home to start the second half of my day.

The afternoon of my "average day" also follows a pretty regimented schedule, but again can vary, depending on the day of the week and how close we are to game day. Normally I'll at least do a core workout along with some more recovery stuff. I usually swim, post-training, twice a week just to get in an extra workout. My afternoons can include a power nap if I'm really feeling the physical tax from training too. I also like to watch a game of soccer every single day while sitting in my Normatec boots, accompanied by my afternoon coffee. I love to study the top players and teams as much as I can. I love to watch soccer. Whether it's recorded game from a European league, a match from the MLS, or a previous game of my own, I'm always watching. I watch one pretty much every single day!

By the time I'm finished with these tasks, it's time to start cooking a meal for dinner before the last segment of my day, which incorporates a recovery session of around 20 minutes where I'll do some more stretching and foam rolling. At this point, the day is coming to a close, the sun has set, and we are into the later hours of the evening. I can take some time to reflect on the day, invest in my relationship, and do whatever I feel is necessary for those final hours of the night.

That is what my typical day looks like. It's pretty regimented and specific, but no matter where I am or how I'm feeling, I try to make sure that I'm maximizing my time. Winning every day. Being productive and efficient, listening to my body, and doing whatever I feel I need to make sure I'm taking care of myself and working towards maximizing my potential. Engaging in these full days of work provide me with a true sense of accomplishment. Whenever I stick to my routine and follow up on my habits, I feel like I make myself a little bit better than I was the day before.

I have all of these items listed on my habit tracker, too. Listed from top to bottom: read, journal, meditate, exercise (train), recovery (boots, stretching, foam rolling, swimming, maintenance work), watch a game, work on my book, etc. The habit tracker has been instrumental in improving my consistency and daily productivity!

James clear, author of "*Atomic Habits*," talks about how even if you make yourself 1% better than you were yesterday, you've won the day. Because as we've talked about, over a long period of time those 1% differences will make all the difference. I highly recommend his book if you're looking for some more in-depth, scientifically proven tips on how you can implement new habits into your routine while eliminating or replacing the bad ones. That book is a game-changer!

"Tiny Changes, Remarkable Results." —James Clear

When I engage with and complete all of my habits for the day, I can get into bed at night feeling awfully productive because I know, with true confidence, that I have put in another day of solid work. I sincerely feel that I've continued to invest in the process that I believe will help me create the life I desire. Although not every single day looks the same, the point is that the majority of my "normal" weekdays follow the format I've laid out above. I live and die by my habits!

I hope you can take something away from my daily routine and process of habits to implement whatever you can into yours. My process revolves around my obsession to learn and to constantly improve. That's one thing I never go a day without! Striving to get better, I am on a relentless schedule in my mind trying to be as resourceful with my time as possible, because I know from experience that the power of habit combined with the power of the compound effect pays dividends in the long run.

The habits you implement will be a catalyst for change. No matter where you're at in life and no matter what you do for a living, your habits and the things you decide to do daily will separate you from everyone else.

I have one other quick piece of advice I'd like to share while we are on the topic of our habits and processes. I feel so lucky, so grateful, and so blessed to be able to say this. To me, what makes engaging with the habits I've incorporated into my routine so special, and what makes my days so compelling and so productive, lies in the fact that *I love what I do*. I'm absolutely infatuated with the grind and I try my best to embrace every part of my day with a heart full of love and gratitude. I find myself feeling the most fulfilled when I go through days with an intense level of work because my work aligns with my passion and purpose!

This leads me back to my point that it's important to find something you love—your *passion*—so that you're aligning your desire to learn from the best with your *vision*. Everything in the BTB process works hand in hand. You need to integrate the habits that shape your life around your vision. In order to ensure that you are finding yourself engaged through the good and bad times, you need to love what you do. If you don't, it'll be much easier to convince yourself out of doing the things you need to do in order to be successful.

I've said it once and I'll say it again... these are the recurring themes that I want to drive and inscribe into your beliefs! Find the desire within your heart, locate your passion, and discipline yourself enough to take the actions necessary to get yourself to where you want to be. Be dedicated to the process when building your habits and engaging with your daily routine and watch how you create everlasting wealth for yourself. Not just material wealth, but an abundance of internal wealth, feeling happiness and joy as you continue to live your life in true harmony with your intentions. I'll leave you with this quote from Aristotle before moving onto the next chapter:

> **"We are what we repeatedly do. Excellence, then, is not an act, but a habit."** —Aristotle

BUILD YOUR
CONFIDENCE

onfidence. Self-belief. Knowing you have what it takes. Believing you have what it takes. That is the essence of true confidence. When confidence is brought up in conversation, it's an area where many people find themselves struggling. Having confidence isn't easy. Building confidence is no easy task either. Believing in yourself when no one else does, is *hard*. However, there are ways in which you can build a heavy-duty, unwavering, and unbreakable sense of self confidence. Once you obtain genuine confidence in yourself, the belief you construct will serve you as arguably your most valuable characteristic in achieving long-term success. That goes for anyone aspiring to be great.

**"Whether you think you can or you think you can't,
you're right."**—Henry Ford

Confidence is a relentless conviction where individuals adopt the certainty in their minds that they can achieve their goals, no matter what obstacles are thrown in their way. Having confidence means that no matter what happens, regardless of the situation, the environment or the circumstances, that you believe that you're equipped to navigate the barriers blocking you from your desired destination. You think that you're more than capable of accomplishing the tasks at hand. That is confidence.

Confidence is a state of mind. And you'll begin to create success in your life when you begin to manage the thoughts between your ears. You have, deep within you, the unlimited power to go on and achieve the things you desire. Everything you need, you already have. The question is... *do you believe it*?

The difference between those who have reached tremendous levels of success and those who haven't isn't some magical pill. Everyone is born equal, but only some are able to adapt a mindset that allows them to prosper. All human beings are made the same way, although our situations and environments may vary.

Robin Sharma says that *"the one who sweats more in training bleeds less in war!"* Whether we are born into poverty, a dysfunctional family, or with a disability, we must choose to play the hands we are dealt regardless. Our self-confidence cannot be reliant on external factors. Those are things we have no control over. We must consciously decide to rise above our adversities. You must consciously choose to armor your mindset by training yourself to believe in who you are as a unique individual. You are someone who can override the odds and limitations pressed on you by society. Take action and believe in what you are doing.

On the other side of the persistent pursuit of maximizing your potential, in spite of all the reasons as to why you can't succeed, lies life's greatest rewards. Life's most precious gift is being reserved for those who believe in themselves enough to chase after their dreams with tenacity, supported by their belief that the process will cultivate the results they wish for. This is the key to being triumphant!

Have you ever heard the saying, "if you don't believe in yourself, then nobody will?" Having a great deal of self-confidence is non-negotiable if you're aspiring to accomplish truly inspiring goals. Achieving greatness has never come easy, not even to the most talented individuals. Why?

Because, the odds of doing great things are always going to be stacked against you. There will be roadblocks, obstacles, and naysayers along the way, all of which, subconsciously, begin to plant seeds of doubt in the back of your mind. Difficult circumstances, seemingly unbeatable barriers, and bumps in the road are going to present themselves and attempt to slow you down; igniting a damaging fire in the process. A fire that sparks questions about what you're doing. You may start to ask yourself things like:

- Is what I am doing worthwhile?
- Is all of the work I am putting in going to pay off?
- If others don't believe I can, why should I try?
- If it didn't work for others, is it going to work for me?
- How do I know this is going to work?
- Am I good enough to accomplish this task?
- How am I going to do this?

The feelings you'll experience that are rooted in self-belief, the emotions that you begin to feel as you continue to knock down the walls that others have built around you, combined with the relentless desire, dedication, and discipline to pursue your dreams will aid you during problematic times. These things will ultimately give you the energy you need to push onto the extra mile.

You can break down the barriers. You can defy the odds. You can accomplish your long-term goals. You can create the life of your dreams because, as Russell Westbrook would say, *"why not*?" Why couldn't you? There is no reason why. There is nothing holding you back other than the thoughts that you're feeding yourself, or the input that others are forcing down your throat. *You* are in control of your thoughts. Your thoughts and beliefs direct your actions. Your actions will then shape your destiny. Everything you need to be the best you can be is *already* inside of you. Harness that power—the power of a choice—and shift your self-limiting beliefs to ones that empower you to make a serious change.

It doesn't matter if I tell you to believe, though, if you don't believe in yourself. You may be someone who's built up years and years worth of pessimistic, disempowering beliefs and thoughts as to why you can't achieve anything of true substance. These disempowering thoughts may be giving you reasons and excuses as to why you weren't born to be great. Reinforcing your self-limiting beliefs, so you remain in your comfort zone, becoming content with mediocrity, and adopting the saddening mindset of *learned helplessness*.

Maybe your friends and family have penetrated your optimistic defense system, forcing you to put down the sword, settle for less than you are capable of, and stop fighting the good fight. We are all susceptible to those dangers. The fear of failing. The possibility of coming out on the other side and having lost the battle. It's all a part of it!

Don't let your *fear of failure* stop you from creating the life you want for yourself. You must dare to fail! Failing from time to time is a sign that you are moving in the right direction because you're demanding more of your-self. Making mistakes means that you're getting out of your comfort zone like we talked about in Chapter 1. Nothing good has ever come from the comfort zone. As you continue to put yourself in uncomfortable situations, you will continue to conquer them. That, in turn, will fuel your confidence. You will tackle one challenge after another and find yourself busting down the doors you once thought were closed, opening yourself up to the infinite possibilities that are available for the taking. Make sure you're one of the ones who takes them!

THE COMMON CONCERN

A common concern in individuals working to acquire *true* confidence in themselves lies at the initial phases of their journey, at the start of the race, and at the sound of the gun. This is actually ironic, because the most important time to believe in yourself is when you're just starting out, because you will not have the results that justify the confidence you need to succeed! Kind of contradictory, isn't it? But it's mandatory! And although it's obviously necessary to maintain your convincing confidence throughout the duration of your journey, it's especially important to have it at the *beginning*. When you are just starting out, taking your first few steps, dipping your toes into unknown waters. It happens to be the most crucial time to obtain unshakeable confidence.

Why do you think this is, if you had to take a guess? I'm going to fill you in as to why I believe having confidence at this stage of your expedition is essential in accomplishing your goals. The reason is, you aren't going to initially have the *results* that people think are required in order to sustain self-confidence.

It's a common misconception that you need to first have results to have confidence in your abilities. What people don't realize, is that they're never ever going to get those results if they don't believe in themselves in the first place! How would you expect to beat out the people who actually have results if you don't believe that you can from the get-go? Yes, you're still going to be early in the process. Yes, you are just beginning the lengthy voyage to becoming your best self. Yes, people are going to tell you that your dreams are crazy, that you're doing too much, working too hard, or that your vision is unrealistic. You'll most likely hear things like:

- It's never going to happen.
- You're better off just doing what everyone else does.
- Just try to fit in, be normal, and be average.

Who are you to think you could be anything more than your environment? Why would you believe you can achieve more than everyone else around you? It's easier just to go with the flow, follow the crowd, and push yourself down the pathway of satisfaction and complacency. Remember, this will all occur at the beginning of your journey. Something interesting will start to take place when you finally reap some of the rewards for thinking outside of the box and pushing yourself to overcome the odds.

It will only be after you finally accomplish something of true substance that the outsiders will begin to support you as someone who is on your side. Once you hit the jackpot, then people will believe you. Then people will understand where your confidence and certainty has come from. But in order to get to that point, you must believe in yourself from the start. Without a self-belief that truthfully knows you'll make it through, persevere, and handle whatever is thrown at you no matter the endeavor, no matter the situation, no matter the external circumstances, you're bound to set yourself up for disappointment. Without confidence, you're increasing the likelihood of coming up short on your long-term goals. If you don't believe in yourself and that you can win the race beforehand, you'll have lost before it's even started. If *you* don't believe that *you* can win, I can promise you that the opponent isn't going to believe in you for you! Don't waste your time comparing. Focus on you, invest in yourself, and fuel your own sense and levels of belief to thrust yourself towards accomplishing the unthinkable.

Ultimately, you have a killer instinct inside of you. You need to trust yourself first. That intuition lies inside of us all. Our gut feeling. Our natural and raw emotions. That little monster inside of us that is dying to break loose of the chains that are holding us back from reaching our greatest heights. Let that confidence off the leash. Stop being timid and worrying about what other people are going to think. You *can* be great, and you *will* create the results you desire as long as you believe that you can in the first place!

No one knows you as well as you know you. Reframe your beliefs behind failure, behind judgment, and behind rejection. Detach the powerful meanings they've constructed in your mind that are putting a cap on your potential. Rather than letting your beliefs and lack of confidence bring you down, use it as fuel to prove everyone wrong who doubts you. Do it for yourself. *You deserve it.* You are amazing and you have what it takes to win in all aspects of your life. Stop limiting yourself. Be confident in who you are as an individual. You are unique and you have a special set of skills that no one else walking the face of this earth has themselves. God made you special. He made you different. He made you, with the intention and purpose of expressing your gifts to the rest of the world. Don't hold back. *Believe*!

YOUR ACTION ITEM. Write down three limiting beliefs you used to have and replace them with three new beliefs that showcase your confidence and the belief you have in yourself.

My Old Limiting Beliefs:

1.

2.

3.

My New Empowering Beliefs:

1.

2.

3.

THE CONSTRUCTION OF CONFIDENCE

As I look back at the early stages of my life, especially the past few years, trying to pinpoint the source of my confidence—the one I have been able to sustain and build from the ground up—is a difficult task. I believe that maintaining my self-belief and finding true confidence in myself was a turning point in my life and has brought me success, not only on the pitch, but off it as well. I can acknowledge the fact that genuine self-confidence begins when you start doing everything in your control to *ensure* your success.

Being confident is something that has come naturally to me as a player. I remember growing up, it didn't matter who lined up across from me on the field, I always believed that I was going to win. I always believed that I was the best one out there. Looking back at my college experience, the confidence I had in myself was still unwavering. Were there times where I questioned myself? Yes. Were there times doubt crept into my mind? Yes. I had to overcome an assortment of different obstacles, but nonetheless, I was confident in my own abilities to get my job done. Now that I'm in the pros, having resolute self-confidence can seem a daunting task when I'm lining up in the tunnel next to guys like Zlatan Ibrahimović, Wayne Rooney, and Luis Nani. Some of the best players of my generation. Guys I grew up idolizing and watching on TV. They've all won big games and a countless number of trophies in the big leagues. Having the confidence to win against those guys is no easy feat! Because you can look at their track record and think "dang, I have no chance at beating a guy who's been there and done that!"

But if I don't believe that my team can win and that I can succeed against that sort of opposition from the start of the game, *I'm not going to have any chance to win at all*! If I don't believe, who's going to? Every fan in the stadium probably thinks that we don't stand a chance. I can't jump on that train and kick myself, too! In order to give myself the best possible chance at success, I need to believe and have confidence in myself that I can, not only compete with them, but *beat* them on the day.

I started my expedition to being a confident person/player by first gaining awareness and becoming conscious of my choices. I learned how to adapt my mindset and label myself as someone who was *constantly trying to learn*. Always striving to improve and shape my craft. Whatever I could do to make me a better person, to make be a better player, to benefit my game, I was all in. The choice was mine to make because I had gained awareness. The awareness in realizing that my daily choices, what I chose to do versus not to do, would produce the results I desired if I sustained them over a long period of time.

As you continue to string together small victories on a day-to-day basis, as a product of your persistent action taking, you will have gained the competitive advantage that is a mental edge.

Confidence isn't something that appears from nothing. Confidence isn't the result of sitting, waiting, and hesitating to take action. Confidence is stemmed through *preparation*. It's preparing yourself accordingly so that when the opportunity you've been waiting for does arise, you'll be fully equipped not to let it pass you by.

> ## "Many people have the will to win, but not many have the will to prepare to win." —Bobby Knight

Think about examples from your past that represent this concept's truth. There is a direct correlation between *preparation* and *confidence*. Imagine an example where you have to do a school project. We've all had projects in school where we've had to give our class a presentation. Surely, all of us went through this at one point or another! I remember I used to always try and get the last time slot in an attempt to delay the process as much as possible.

Here's the part where preparation and confidence come into play. Have you ever noticed that the presentations that ran smoothly, the one's where you received an A+ grade on, are the ones that you practiced and prepared for? I've experienced both cases. One of being prepared and a few where I absolutely winged it.

During the times I prepared accordingly, when I read my notecards in the mirror to make sure my speech was on point. Set up a PowerPoint with pretty colors and pictures to help portray my point of view. I had always done well. There were times when I went in with no preparation at all. Came up with everything on the spot. No preparation, no notecards, no PowerPoint presentations.

Yeah, the final grade I received was much different, sure. But, where I noticed the biggest difference were in my feelings before I even presented! I noticed, how during the times I had prepared, I was calm, composed, and most importantly, *confident*. On the flip side, if I knew I wasn't prepared, I would find myself feeling nervous, tense, and clammy. It was during the presentations where I took my time and prepared to the best of my ability that proved to be my best performances of all. I stepped up in front of my classmates, as confident as ever, thinking that I could deliver the results I wanted and blew the project out of the water! Has that ever happened to you? To this day, I try and replay that example in my mind when trying to find the will to prepare to win. I try and study the details. I work on finding tasks and working in areas that my competitors may not be paying attention to. That will ultimately give me the confidence I need to succeed!

You have to try to take advantage of the small specific areas where others may be missing out. Thinking this way could trigger a domino effect that will start to pour over into many other areas of your career and life.

When I started to stay after training and put in hours of extra work, get in additional strengthening, watch extra film, and try to locate the parts of my game where I could progress. That was when I understood how those were the actions and key components to growing, what is now, my resolute self-confidence. It's all in your preparation.

If you know in your mind and heart that you're taking control of every factor that is in your vision and putting in the work, you will build confidence in knowing that you can handle whatever the circumstance may be. Every decision you make is made with a purpose. No matter how big or small. Going the extra mile to make sure that you're prepared for whatever situation arises because it's going to give yourself the confidence you need to win. No matter the condition, no matter the disorders and chaos going on in a game, or in the office; the quality of your *preparation* is what will supply you with the belief that you can handle whatever is required to make sure that you get the job done.

I know from experience that it can be hard to believe in yourself when you're forced to deal with a task that you've never dealt with before. Truth be told once again, confidence comes from the feeling of preparation that we have been talking about, so when you feel unprepared, the result is shaky self-confidence. All you can do is control what you can and make sure that you are well primed regardless! That is the only component that you *can* control. You can't control the external. You can, however, take full responsibility for making sure you are mentally, physically, and emotionally prepared for the ride. If you put in the hours to prepare yourself, if you work harder than the rest, if you do what you can to separate yourself, you will plant the seeds of self-confidence needed to grow and create the life you've always dreamed of.

Follow the BTB process and you will create a new form of confidence that you may have never experienced before. Commit yourself to *learning from the best*, *see your vision* clearly, locate your *desires*, be unapologetically *disciplined* and *dedicated*, and *develop empowering habits*. Get your hands dirty and put in the work. It's the only way to build the confidence you need to succeed.

THE COMMON MISCONCEPTION

A common misconception that pertains to self-confidence is its relationship with one word... *cocky*. Cockiness, also known as arrogance or being conceited, is not what I am talking about when I refer to self-belief and/or confidence. Being cocky will not lead you in the right direction. The character traits of someone who is cocky and arrogant don't mix in well with the recipe for someone who has *real confidence*. Here are some of the key differences:

COCKINESS	CONFIDENCE
▪ Insecure	▪ Secure
▪ Close-Minded	▪ Open-Minded
▪ External	▪ Internal

"Confidence can get you to the top. Cockiness is thinking you're already there." —Stephen Curry

There is an extraordinary difference between confidence and cockiness. When you represent the traits of someone who is cocky, you feel the need to tell the world about how great you are. Cocky people love to talk about themselves and feel entitled to share how amazing their accomplishments and successes are with all of their peers. In my opinion, cockiness is a mask for insecurity. Those who are cocky don't have real confidence in themselves, so they use a façade of arrogance to cover up their truths. Talk, talk, and talk some more. Cockiness is commonly revealed by those who love to chat about their own winnings.

When you are truly confident in yourself, you don't have to tell anyone anything. Confident individuals know that rather than telling others about what they've done, or can do, they can instead, *show* them. The *results* will speak volumes for themselves.

When someone is cocky and feels the need to talk the talk, it may seem like they're showcasing a great deal of confidence because they speak so highly of themselves. The sheep may believe it and be amused by their underlying insecurities, but the reality, is talking a big game unfortunately reveals the sad truth of chinks in the armor. If you feel that you must show-case and talk-up your victories to your colleagues, it may be because, deep down, you know that you don't feel like what you have actually done is good enough for someone else's standards or approval. Therefore, you seek out the praise from those around you. Confidence is shown when you are walking the walk. Doing. Acting. Walking... *not talking.* Having confidence speaks for itself.

When you are confident in who you are, confident in what you do, and confident in what you represent, you don't need external attention because everything you need, you already have, internally. Your belief isn't contingent on what others think of you or your accomplishments. What other people say or believe has no effect on what you know about yourself. You believe in yourself, no exceptions. When you have that true confidence, nothing else matters. Nothing can stand in your way! Be confident, but don't be cocky.

People who think they know it all can also fall into the category of someone who is cocky. A common trait of someone who is falsely confident is that they believe they are always right and that they know what's best. They aren't open to outside counsel or advice. Confident people are secure with themselves and know that the knowledge of others helps their cause as a whole. *Confident individuals are more concerned with what is right rather than who is right.* Be confident in who you are, but never block out anyone else's insight by letting your ego get in the way. Cockiness goes hand in hand with a closed, limited mind. Confidence ignites an open mind and allows you take in all insights in perspectives to help further your understanding, making your confidence even stronger than before. Represent yourself in a way that aligns with your values!

"Anything is possible once you believe you are worthy of achieving it." —Jason Pockrandt

Confidence is non-negotiable on the pathway to success. Being confident means that you're secure and proud of who you are and what you represent. Being confident showcases itself when you commit yourself to preparing to win. When you know that you've worked harder, paid more attention to the details, and studied more intentionally, you will obtain the unwavering belief in your abilities because you'll know that you've done what is required and expected to succeed. *You can write your own future.*

When you put yourself into practice mode, more than the competition, and shape your craft relentlessly, that groundwork fuels the conviction you'll feel in knowing that you can accomplish your goals. You'll be able to adapt to your surroundings and be resilient through whatever comes your way. Tim Grover, in his book *"Relentless,"* talks about how you'll know when someone is straight-up confident in themselves by how they handle certain situations. When everyone else presses the panic button and doesn't have the training or preparation to revert to, the individuals who prepare will be able to stay calm, collected, and as cool as the other side of the pillow, knowing they can handle whatever the situation is and still *win*.

Know deep in your heart, feel in your soul, and believe in your mind that *you got this*! You can handle the job on your own. No handouts. No panic. No tension. No worry. Just faith and belief. Whether you are on the playing field, in a business meeting, or giving a presentation. Whatever aspect of life or field you're in, being prepared is what ultimately gives you the confidence necessary to go on and fulfill your wildest dreams.

You need to be confident in yourself. Believe in what you are doing and know with inevitability, that you're worth every single one of the pennies you invest in yourself. Preparing yourself accordingly will help you sustain unshakeable confidence. Start by building good habits. Instill an efficient daily routine where you are making the most out of your days and getting the most out of yourself. All of these actions, compounded over time and added together, will result in definite self-belief. You'll be able to shatter your old limitations and become more than you ever imagined possible.

Naysayers want you to be as average as they are by downplaying your dreams and comparing your situation to their own. Find it within yourself to believe that you were made for something more. Don't let anyone take that belief from you.

Always be solution-oriented, instead of focusing on the problems and the things you cannot control. Odds are just numbers so don't let them concern you. John C. Maxwell lays it out extremely well when he talks about our needs to shift the way we think. Change your thought patterns from "can I?" to *"how can I?"* See yourself achieving impeccable things and have the belief that you have the potential to do so.

"Find the answer to every problem, not the problem to every answer." —Barbara Johnson

Understand that when you develop a hunger to do whatever it takes—and I mean *whatever* it takes—to get what you want; nothing can stop you. You must believe that there isn't anything or anyone who can hold you back. That is the truth, especially when you are in a state of indestructible confidence!

If you are determined to get what you want, you'll believe you can do it. It's as simple as that. It is essential to adopt this mindset of resilience if you want to be successful. You need to be persistent through trials and push through until you see the light at the end of the tunnel. The only limitations we are given in this lifetime are the ones that we impose on ourselves in our own minds. When you are confident in who you are as an individual, you are unstoppable.

When I am on the field and I am playing in a state of full and complete confidence, there is nothing that can get in the way of me hitting my targets and goals. I'm only going to continue to prepare myself to the highest degree so that I can continue to add to my foundation. I'm going to keep working to prove people wrong, to fulfill my dreams, and to surpass the expectations that I've laid out for myself. We as individuals are in control of the way we think, of the thoughts we choose to pay attention to, and of the beliefs we choose to adapt. Some years ago, I made the choice to believe in myself against all odds. To *Bet On Myself...* it was the best decision I've ever made.

"Mental toughness means you don't believe the hype when you win, and you don't fall apart when you lose." —Tim Grover

The belief that you cannot be stopped and the certainty that you will develop by doing what is required to get to the place you desire, will be because you have sacrificed the time to prepare yourself accordingly. That, my friends, is what ultimately will give you the buoyancy and assurance you need to defy the limits!

IT'S ALL IN THE STATE OF MIND —Walter D. Wintle

If you think you are beaten, you are,
If you think that you dare not, you don't,
If you'd like to win, but you think you can't, It's almost certain you won't.
If you think you'll lose, you've lost,
For out in the world you'll find Success begins with a fellow's will—
It's all in the state of mind.

Full many a race is lost
 ere even a step is run,
And many a coward fall ere
even his work's begun,
Think big, and your deeds will grow;
Think small, and you'll fall behind;
Think that you can, and you will—
It's all in the state of mind.

If you think you are out-classed, you are;
You've got to think high to rise;
You've got to be sure of yourself before
You ever can win a prize,
Life's battles don't always go
To the stronger or faster man;
But soon or late the man who wins
Is the man who thinks he can.

BECOME DRIVEN BY FEAR

Being afraid or being fearful is portrayed as an unpleasant emotion caused by the belief that someone or something is dangerous, likely to cause pain, or is a threat. Based on that definition, we then note our *feelings of fear* as something to avoid. We live in a society where we are taught to downplay our fears and we learn that we should step up against them.

However, all of us inevitably deal with the emotions of fear, anxiety, or anger in some form throughout the course of our lives. How can we learn to channel these emotions and use them in a way that empowers us and pushes us to become our best selves, in spite of these feelings?

An important element to understand about the individuals who reach great levels of success in their lifetimes is *not* that they don't experience fear. Everyone does. Fear is inevitable, especially when you're approaching the boundaries of your comfort zone. However, the people who succeed find a way to direct their fears in a fashion that empowers them rather than letting their fears paralyze them. Most people view fear as negative, an emotion to avoid at all cost. To most, fear is something to evade and escape. What comes to mind when you think of the things that you're afraid of?

Now, I want to clarify what kind of fears I am talking about. What I'm referring to when bringing up the topic of fear as an emotion is the deeper, internal, crippling fears. That can vary from things like the fear of failure.

The fear of success. The fear of trying and not succeeding. The fear of letting people down. The fear of what other people are going to think. All of which, by the way, are going to paralyze you from taking action and place a massive cap on your personal power.

As human beings, it's within our genetic nature to run the other way if we believe that something will cause us to feel pain. That fear—the avoidance of pain—causes us to run in the opposite direction. We've been taught over the years to hide our pain. To numb ourselves at the very thought of experiencing emotions that bring us fear. How will we then grow as individuals? How do you learn to walk if, at first, you don't fall down trying?

Avoiding our fears and allowing them to paralyze us from taking risks is a one-way ticket to leading a life of mediocrity and complacency. We need to learn how to live purposeful lives in spite of the presence of fear because those feelings are foreseeable. By not facing your fears, by not taking control of them, and by not directing them towards something useful, there will be serious mental, physical, emotional, and spiritual consequences.

STEP 1: ACCEPT YOUR FEARS

The first step to overcoming and facing the things that frighten you is *accept* that they are there. Understand that what you are feeling is completely normal. No one is fearless. *No one*! However, the best of the best have learned how to act, regardless of their feelings of fears. They don't let their fears stop them from chasing their dreams. They don't allow their fears to take over their lives and put a halt to doing anything productive. Yes, we all feel fear. But it is our ability to go through the flames of fear, regardless of our feelings about it. That will provide us with life's ultimate gift. The one that is waiting for the brave individuals who face their fears straight on and tackle them with true conviction.

STEP 2: LABEL YOUR FEARS BY WRITING THEM DOWN!

I would like to introduce you to an exercise that I think would be useful in trying to pinpoint what exactly it is that you're afraid of. As you take a step forward toward the person that you want to become, you need to start by locating those fears and understanding them right now.

Let's figure out what might be holding you back from the abundance that is waiting for you on the other side of boldness. The whole purpose of this activity is to help you gain awareness. That is how we start. You need to understand what it is that you're avoiding. Once we find the root cause, we will then be able to learn how to redirect those fears in a methodology that will motivate you. If you struggle with finding and pinpointing the root cause of your fears, doubts, or insecurities, I'd highly recommend going and talking to a professional to help reveal some of those truths to you. Whether that be a counselor, or a therapist it's something I think is incredibly helpful. I have been going to counseling for years, ever since my parent's divorce, and it's been one of the most instrumental practices I've been committed to. Anyhow, let's get back to the exercise!

Write down three things that you may be afraid of. Things that are truly holding you down. It's time to break free from those ties so that you can step into and become the best version of yourself. Close your eyes and take a few minutes if you have to. Pause for a second and please, please, please don't skip this step! Understanding what it is that may be stopping you from taking action is a decisive component to the BTB approach!

YOUR ACTION ITEM. Think about what causes you to feel the emotion of fear. What is it that is starving you of the influence you need to act towards your life's most desired outcomes?

1.

2.

3.

> **"The pathway to your greatest potential is through your biggest fear."** —Craig Groeschell

Congratulations! You've just taken a BIG step in the right direction by writing down your fears on paper. You can see them with your own eyes. You're now aware of some things that may be holding you back. And with awareness comes power because now you're the one who is in control. Take a look at your deep level fears. Redirect them in a way that inspires you to be the best you can be. That is the next step! Let's take a look at how we can do that right now. Redirecting and reframing your fears in a way that fuels you rather than drains you is going to allow you to harness your fears and make them work for you rather than against you! Let's keep going and keep pushing upwards.

STEP 3: REDIRECT YOUR FEARS

Redirecting your fears will drastically change the results and feelings you'll experience throughout your life. Implementing this concept into my life by changing my belief system, inspired me to perceive my fears in a positive fashion and live my life to the fullest instead of allowing my fears to rob me of my joy. Rather than letting my fears control me, I have been able to give myself a new role as the captain of my own life, rather than the passenger. I came to a point where I knew there was more and that something had to be done.

Instead of viewing my fears as something to avoid, I've familiarized myself with them. I've restructured my mind to see the emotion of fear as an empowering message. When my expected feelings of fear arise, I'm able to step back and understand that those feelings are a result of my body and mind sending me a message.

You may be thinking, "um... *hello*? If I'm coming face-to-face with fear, I must be doing something wrong. I'd better turn around! I better stop what I'm doing to avoid the possibility of experiencing pain." This is where we need to resupply our *belief systems*. Subconsciously, we've always believed that fear is something we want to avoid, right? Wrong! *Redirect* your subconscious mind and the beliefs deep down in your core. When you experience fear, the little voice inside you must start saying, *"I am on the right track."*

Fact. When you're feeling fearful, that actually means that you're moving in the right direction! Learn to see fear this way and you too can be on your way to changing your destiny. Adapt that perspective. See your fears as an action signal that is telling you this: "I am being challenged. I am pushing myself beyond my comfort zone. I am moving beyond my previously perceived limitations. I am *growing*!"

Becoming complacent and comfortable is playing a dangerous game. By not stretching your boundaries or challenging yourself, by staying right where you are, you're giving fear all of the power over you. In his book, *"The 15 Invaluable Laws of Personal Growth,"* John C. Maxwell explains what he refers to as "the law of the rubber band." He illuminates that we have the capability to grow and stretch ourselves, much like a rubber band, and that we should live our lives much like a rubber band. So, allow me to pose a few questions in relation to this law. How do you use a rubber band? When is it at its best? When are you maximizing the potential of the rubber band? Well, the rubber band only works if it stretches!

Stretching yourself beyond your comfort zone and by embracing and facing the things that you may have once been afraid of can be life altering. When you're pushing yourself and driving beyond the limitations you once knew, you are allowing yourself the chance to be great and to aspire for the things that you once thought were out of reach.

By now we've driven home how important it is to make yourself aware of the things you fear the most. Learning what it is that is stopping you from chasing your dreams with scorching passion. We've also talked about how important it is to redirect your fears as an empowering message that you're taking the right steps towards achieving greatness. As we progress through understanding and redirecting our feelings about our fears, the next step is a hefty one. We're now going to dive into one of the most profound tools in this book: being driven by our fears...

STEP 4: BECOME DRIVEN BY YOUR FEARS

When you are driven by a strong, powerful fear, it will push you to the next level. Fear can be an extremely empowering tool when embraced in the correct manner. However, what you choose to attach to your fears can either aid you or destroy you. This can be seen similarly to our understanding of the concept of *linking our desires* that we covered in previous chapters.

Fear can serve you as one of two things. First and foremost, it can be an awfully disempowering limitation that can hold you back from achieving everything you desire. Or, conversely, it can be an indisputable motivating factor that propels you towards maximizing your potential and achieving everything you've ever wanted. Be it material wealth, harmony, inner peace, or a life full of joy, you can have it all if you learn how to be driven by your fears. It all depends on how you perceive it.

Everyone feels fear and has things they are afraid of, right? As we mentioned earlier, feeling fear at one point or another is unavoidable. But have you ever asked yourself, what are your preconceived emotions about fear? Do you know if they're helping or hurting your chances at living out your dreams? Are you running from your fears and avoiding them, or are you grabbing ahold of them and using them to your advantage?

> **"Fear is not the problem; it's your reaction to fear that leads to toxicity and self-sabotage. You can choose to eliminate your reactivity to fear. If you choose to hang on to that reaction, that is your free will."** —Sherianna Boyle

Modifying the beliefs that you've built up over the years and learning to appreciate the emotion of fear, will help you recognize your *reactions* to fear, so that you can better assist yourself in the future when experiencing similar emotions. Recognize that when you are feeling fear, your body is, again, sending you a signal that you've moved beyond your comfort zone. You're moving in the right direction.

Once you figure out how to use the feelings that you associate with fear as fuel, you become unstoppable. It all depends on what fears you're allowing to creep into your mind that end up dominating your thoughts. Yes, we're all going to experience fear on the road to personal mastery. But what if I told you there was a way to use your greatest fear as your greatest asset? What if I told you that by creating fear and linking massive pain to it, that you could motivate yourself to turn your vision into reality? What do you link to your fears and what do those associations force you to do?

Being driven and fueled by fears can give you an overriding energy when trying to find the proper motivation to take action toward accomplishing your long-term goals. Let's go through some tips on how you can learn to use this power to your advantage. I think I can best portray my perspective by sharing an example through personal experience.

In my case, I have learned how to be driven by my fears in both my life and my career. Learning how to be driven by my fears has become exceedingly helpful in understanding my feelings of fear as a whole and using them in a way that supports my dreams.

Let me take this a step further now. Here's how I use my fears as motivation.

First, I take myself out of my current situation and try to see the future version of myself. Being that I'm in the middle of my professional soccer career, the initial step is being able to zoom out from the present moment and fast forward to the time where my career may be coming to a close. By taking myself out of my current circumstance, I'm able to come face-to-face with my biggest fear. The fear of not reaching my potential when it comes to the end of my playing days. The fear of not maximizing my time and not following my pursuit to become the best version of myself. When it's time to "hang up the boots," I don't want to have any regrets.

You may be thinking this is a pointless exercise and you may not understand its purpose quite yet but bear with me! What I have found to be so helpful in motivating me to take massive action *right now* is what I have been able to link my own fears to. I use them to drive me today and every day. What I have revealed to be my biggest fear, at this point of my life, is to come to the tail end of my career and be able to look back on my earlier days and think to myself:

"Damn, I wish I would have put more time into my game."
"I could have applied myself a little more in this area."
"I regret not doing more to ensure I made the most out of my career."

Tony Robbins talks about the two kinds of pain that can be experienced based off of every decision we make. This concept is revolutionary and can literally change your life.

THE PAIN OF DISCIPLINE VS. THE PAIN OF REGRET

The pain of *discipline* (the immediate pain that comes from doing the things you know you should do but don't want to), or the pain of *regret* (the delayed pain you'll feel when you wish you would have done the things you know you should have done). And as for me, I don't do regret.

"You only regret the things you didn't do."
—Michael Curtiz

I'd much rather face the pain that comes through being disciplined than live with the pain of regret. I know that would haunt me for the rest of my life. Therefore, when I'm able to put myself in my own shoes, 10 years in the future, my biggest fear would be to look back on my earlier years in the game, knowing that I didn't do everything I could to ensure my own success. I sincerely don't know how I would handle that possibility down the road.

That is how I can push myself past many of my colleagues, *by using fear as the primary fuel*. The amount of pain that I have been able to link to that specific feeling of possible regret, the amount of fear that I have built up in my mind to reaching that moment, has helped me take action towards creating the things I want *right now*. I can only imagine the heartache and remorse that I would feel and have to live with for the rest of my life and I don't want to leave any possibility of that happening. The thought of it makes me crazy and forces me to do what is required to make sure that I don't have to experience that kind of pain!

Ed Mylett, serial entrepreneur and ultra-successful businessman always talks in his podcast about a similar comparison he makes in his own life. He talks about how his biggest fear is a fictional scenario, where he meets the best version of himself and that person is a complete stranger. That is some *powerful* stuff!! That's what prompts him to work so hard and improve himself every single day, to ensure that he's done everything in his control to be able to look back on his life with complete contentment in knowing he gave his all in everything he did. That is how you use fear to motivate you and to drive you.

I find this kind of thinking to be extremely beneficial. What we link our fears and pain to can either stop us entirely from taking any action at all or drive us to new maxims. I can relate to this method of living. The only way to avoid that immense pain of possible future regret would come from knowing that I had done everything I could to win each and every day. Having directed my focus on controlling things that were in my control and having pushed myself to the max with the ultimate purpose of trying to get to my desired destination. That's the only way I know I can look back on my life with no regret and feel fulfilled. By making the most out of each individual day. Having that fear in the back of my mind drives me every day to take immense action, ultimately acting as an additional energy source to my self-discipline.

The fear that drives me is not only the foundation of my discipline, but the groundwork for my confidence as well. Because by using fear as a driving force in my day-to-day life, I find myself taking the actions that are necessary to give myself the sense of preparation that confidence stems from, like we talked about earlier. Recognizing and utilizing that fear of regret can be an unrelenting motivating factor in pushing you toward developing the things that you really want. Realize the power in being driven by your fears. Learn to use them before they use you. Take advantage of this concept and find a way to reframe your beliefs so that you too can live out your dreams!

The key is to identify that fear of regret *right now*. Put yourself in the shoes of who you believe you can become someday. Think of the things that you want to do. Feel the pain that would colonize your heart if you didn't take action towards becoming the best version of yourself today! Manifest your vision and bring fear on your side.

> **"The reward you'll receive as you fully express
> your strengths and gifts isn't only the product of
> your heroic efforts. It's who you'll become by advancing
> through the fire of your fears and the heat of your trials
> along the process to mastery."** —Robin Sharma

Bet On Yourself every single time, every day of the week! Know with certainty, because you've given everything to the process, that you'll be ready for whatever opportunities come your way. Know it. Feel it. Believe it. God is good, the universe has your back, and the process is *real*.

DON'T BE A SHOULDA, COULDA, WOULDA...

Growing up, I remember hearing something from an older generation that really stood out to me. I had always heard stories of how people think they could've been this or how someone they know could've, would've, or should've been that. They really believed that they should have been something that ultimately and unfortunately, they are not. Truthfully, those stories planted seeds in my heart that repeated this message: don't be another "shoulda, coulda, woulda" story! With my dream of becoming a professional soccer player, I did not want to be one of those people who went around telling the youth about how I could have been a pro. I was legitimately scared of being a shoulda/woulda/coulda type of guy. I've linked too much pain to that experience to ever let that happen. Those stories have inspired me to this day!

Any fear with a strength of that degree will push you to work for the things you truly believe you can accomplish. Take full responsibility for your life. That includes where you've been, where you're currently at, and where you're going. Your future is dependent on what you do now. Invite fear onto your side and harness its power to create amazing things for yourself. Make the choice to be driven by your fears and do something today that you will thank yourself for later.

So, ask yourself this: what can you do in this very moment that you will be grateful for one day as you reflect upon your life? It might be something you don't necessarily want to do, like starting the habit of waking up before the sun rises or going to the gym, or facing the temporary pain of quitting your job so that you can chase after dreams of your own. It's okay for those decisions to be hard and for those choices to be difficult to make. The most successful people in our lives have separated themselves because of their uncanny ability to do the things that most others don't want to do. Someday, you'll be able to look back and think, "man, am I glad I took immediate action all those years ago to do X, Y, and Z, because the payoff has been outstanding."

Don't let your fear of failing, fear of what others think, or fears of anything else stop you from creating the life you long for! The *only* thing you should fear is not maximizing your full potential! No one else is going to bet on you, no one else is going to do the work for you, so you have to bet on yourself and jump into the ring and fight on your own! Take the chance to reap the rewards from getting into a grind. Because this life has so many beautiful things to offer. Whatever you desire, whatever success and wealth you wish to acquire, you can have. Everything you do, and everything you decide not to do is a choice. It's in your hands. You have the power to make a decision that can change the course of your entire life.

BRING FEAR ON YOUR SIDE

In my field of professional sports, whenever I struggle with finding the motivation to work out on a gloomy day or to get in some extra work at the training field; going back and finding that place where I can put myself in my own shoes 10 years down the line becomes extremely inspirational. During those times, I try and refer to my well-expanded toolbox and find a way to drive myself with the fear of regret in order to get myself to take action right then and there. Even as a professional athlete, where physical training directly corresponds to my occupation. I sometimes struggle with finding the energy and strength to do extra work. It's certainly not easy to go the extra mile, especially when your body is depleted from the resources and energy it needs to function! However, it's the extra stuff that will allow me to separate myself from everyone else. Therefore, I have linked more pain to the feeling of not doing any extra work (because I feel like I'm cheating myself) than to the literal pain I will actually endure while doing the additional training itself.

The exercise that corresponds to *being driven by your fears* has allowed me to act in accordance with what I believe will bring me contentment down the road. That relief in knowing that I will have nothing to look back on and feel bad about because maybe doing just that little bit more will make all the difference in the end. One thing I know for sure is that the pain I will have later on, knowing I hadn't run that extra mile or done that extra rep, will haunt me far more than the pain I will experience while running the actual extra mile itself.

I've talked about how you need to learn from the best, in order to be the best. I've talked about how having a long-term vision for yourself and speaking your desires into existence helps bring them to reality. I've talked about how impactful it is to have good habits and the importance of running an effective daily routine. I've talked about the significance of locating and linking your deepest desires, in correlation with the power of being disciplined and dedicated to your passion. I've talked about having the unshakeable confidence to believe in yourself throughout the adversity you will face on the road less taken, all with the purpose of giving yourself a competitive advantage.

Adopting these perspectives and belief systems will all help you get to your desired destination. Being driven by your fears can be the *prime force* that will give you the momentum you need to take action in every area of your life. Allowing yourself to be driven by what you're most afraid of will push you to take an insane amount of action. I've seen it work in my own life and I've experienced the pay off in the short-term. Can you imagine what the results can be if you persistently execute this principle over an extended period of time?

I've said it once and I'll say it again, *the progress gives back*. When you find yourself using all of these philosophies to take action today by being consistent over time, you will find yourself accomplishing the unexpected, unthinkable, and unimaginable. That is, to everyone but yourself. You'll always have known that you were bound for greatness because of the steps you've taken over years and years in the dark. It's only a matter of time before your light shines and beams through all the walls of perceived limitations. When you notice this concept working in your life, you will find yourself looking for any and every area where you are able to take just the slightest advantage over the opposition.

Being driven by your fears is an unmatched component and it will push you to be more disciplined, confident, and dedicated than you ever thought conceivable. Using fear to your advantage can inspire you, lead you, and drive you to have good habits, which we know that when compounded over time, create monumental results. Or it can paralyze you from taking any action at all by stopping you from trying and leaving you to feel nothing but sorrow and disappointment as you stare regret straight in the face when your time comes to an end.

Embrace your fears. Feel the future regret you could face if you don't take action right now. Start small and slowly progress towards your bigger goals. Soon, through authentic practice, you will be able to master this skill once and for all. Program it into your hardwiring and you will find it to be the missing key that you've needed to open the doors that lead you straight to the life you've always dreamed of. One of the most important pieces to the puzzle.

Learn to love your fears. Use them, be driven by them, and they will force you to take the steps that will result in the construction of an unwavering belief in yourself, because *you* are going to be doing everything that is required to get yourself to where you want to go. That is power. That is potential being used. Fear is going to be a part of the game whether you like it or not... better get it on your side and use it before it uses you.

YOUR ACTION ITEM. Write down three ways that you are going to use your fears to act now:

1.

2.

3.

ACCEPT
NO EXCUSES

7

An excuse is defined as *"an attempt to lessen the blame attaching to fault, in a seek to defend or justify."* When I take a look at that dictionary given definition, the key words that jump off the page are *"attaching to fault."*

One of the most common issues we encounter in our lives, more often than not, is that people try to attach blame to *something out of their control.* Something external. Something that is not themselves. We are always looking for a way out and a reason as to why things happen the way they do. By creating excuses in our minds and not holding ourselves accountable, we are trying to lessen our feelings of pain associated with our realities. Taking full responsibility for where you are in life could be a tough pill to swallow if you aren't where you'd like to be. As a matter of fact, it's one of the hardest things to do. It's much easier to blame someone or something else, right? As individuals, we often lack the ability to take full accountability for where we are in our lives.

Why does everyone want to point fingers? In our current world, we're taught to shift the responsibility for not achieving our goals toward some external factor. While it may be true that you can't control what happens to you in your life, you can always control how you respond. That in itself is a conscious decision.

Stephen Covey talks about an interesting principle in *"The 7 Habits of Highly Effective People."* Think about the word "responsibility" for a second. In his well-renowned book, Stephen further breaks down the word responsibility into two pieces, "response-ability." In other words, our ability to respond. How fascinating is that when you take a second to really think about it? We truly don't have control over what happens to us in our lives. But Stephen describes how we can always control our ability to respond *positively* to the unexpected turbulences that happen to us. I absolutely love that.

How would you rate your ability to respond? When you evaluate your own life in attempt to understand why you maybe haven't achieved the things you want just yet. How do you perceive the reason as to why? Do you think it's always someone else's fault? Or potentially because of an external circumstance that forced you off your ways? Our capability to throw aside excuses, persist forward, and respond in a supportive fashion will bring us the success we desire most.

In the most extreme cases there are uncontrollable situations that arise. One example would be a prospering professional athlete who faces a career-ending injury. In such an experience, we can still control how we respond and react to these unfortunate life occurrences. Even under the most tragic circumstances, we must understand that we always have the power to see it from a perspective that will empower us to make the most out of whatever cards we're dealt.

You have to try with every ounce of your energy not to let something out of your control dictate the course of your destiny. If you were to encounter such a unique case, your ideas and visions of what you wanted may need to alter course, but the bumps in the road can be no reason to stop you entirely. You can always veer towards a different path. There's always another route. Even though you're adjusting your approach and adapting to what occurs in your life, you can never use external circumstances as an excuse! The only reason why you wouldn't be able to live a life of abundance would be by allowing an external situation to control you negatively.

Easier said than done for sure. If you *say* you want to achieve tremendous things, but you're not quite there yet for whatever reason, what are you doing *right now* to change that? Are you controlling everything that is in your control? That includes your work ethic, your attitude, and your effort!

> **"There are two primary choices in life: To accept conditions as they exist or accept responsibility for changing them."**
> —Dennis Waitley

Reality check, my friends. You're going to be in big trouble along the journey towards your goals if you don't find a way to take full accountability and extreme ownership for where you are. You must, and I repeat you *must*, 100% all the time, on every day of the week, take accountability for where you are in your life. That is the one and only way you can accomplish anything of true substance.

TRUE POWER

Now let me stop being so harsh and blunt for a minute so that I can bring this back around full circle. I'm preaching the importance of not making excuses for a good reason. Because once you own your response-ability with true conviction, something wonderful happens. *You gain clarity.* You've come to a *true* understanding that if you're the only reason why you are where you are, *you're giving yourself all of the power.* The power to choose a better future and a new direction.

This idea is so empowering because it provides you with the understanding that you can affect tomorrow by what you do today. If you take full responsibility for your past and present, it allows you to affect the outcome of your future. *You* are the only person who can get yourself out of tough situations. *You* are the only person who can create wealth for yourself. *You* are the only person who is going to work to make your dreams a reality. No one is going to come and hand your desired outcomes to you on a silver platter! You must believe that you can change any situation or circumstance. That is magnified when you embrace your current situation and never make excuses.

Simple enough, right? It's not too hard for me to sit here and say from behind my computer screen. At the end of the day I don't know what you've been through, where you've been, or how your past has affected your life. I realize that. I am also completely aware that this is not an easy idea to implement into your life. I still find it hard to apply in every aspect of my own life, but that's a part of it!

Not blaming someone or something else is never going to be the easiest thing to do. Although it is insanely difficult to truly own every aspect of your past and present, I also know that it is fundamental to long-term success. Taking this level of ownership is, like I said, a tall task. It's problematic to look in the mirror when you're disappointed with where you are and take full accountability for your current situation. It's a hard smack in the face and can bring you a lot of pain. But that is the only way through it. It is the *only way through it*!

If you're running away from the pain of your reality, I really want to encourage you to face it with tenacity and own every last bit of it. Because unless you confront your pain, unless you take an honest look at your reality of not being where you want to be, unless you truthfully hold yourself accountable, you're going to continue running in circles of avoidance. You're going to continue making poor excuses. You must truly believe that you are where you are in life because of how you've reacted to or dealt with the uncontrollable situations that have happened all throughout your life. Tony Robbins repeats this message constantly in his books and podcasts: *"Life does not happen to you; it happens for you."*

EVERYTHING HAPPENS FOR A REASON

Understanding this concept is non-negotiable if you are to succeed and fulfill the vision you have laid out for yourself. Life happens. Shit happens. Sometimes it might be good, and sometimes it might be bad. You can't control that part so don't waste your time.

I've mentioned earlier that in order to change your reality, you need to alter your expectations because they're the root of disappointment and sorrow. With that being said, you need to expect struggle. Expect adversity. Expect to face difficult conditions. There will probably come a time where you want to quit. Where you want to throw in the towel. If you choose to go that route, fine. But don't play the blame game and point fingers. Don't allow yourself to say, "I never made it because that one thing happened." Excuses, along with self-imposed perceived limitations, are the only things that will squeeze the life out of your dreams.

The most successful people that we know are those who have been resilient throughout turbulent waters. Who've armored themselves with a mindset that no matter what happens, they know that they're going to make it work. No matter how hard it is to take the blame at times, regardless of the pain they face from owning their problems straight up, they take it upon themselves to turn their lives around. Then *they do it*. Taking full accountability for your life supports the recurring important theme of getting out of your comfort zone.

Have you ever heard the saying, "if you want something you've never had, you must do something that you've never done?" I was listening to an audio book during my travel time a few years back that really inspired me. I came across an awfully interesting concept that John C. Maxwell talks about in his book, "*The 15 Invaluable Laws of Personal Growth.*" John talks about how *growth stops completely when you lose the tension between where you are and where you want to be.* In order to push yourself to places you've never been and in order to maximize your full potential, you must get comfortable with being uncomfortable. You do that by stopping the excuses. By cutting out the disempowering reasons that are putting a treacherous cap on your capabilities.

THE VICTOR VS. THE VICTIM MINDSET

Obtaining a victor's mindset will help you gain leverage towards taking full control of your life. You need to try and develop a victor's mindset rather than the maintaining the typical victim's mindset.

Let me provide you with a few of the key distinctions between the two frames of mind. Victors are solution oriented. The Victors win by holding themselves accountable. Victors always finds a way by taking matters into their own hands. On the other hand, victims point fingers and blame external causes for their shortcomings. Instead of looking internally, the victims believe that no matter what they do, they will always fall victim to the external circumstances that life provides.

VICTIMS	VICTORS
- Blame others	- Blame themselves
- Take no responsibility	- Holds themselves accountable
- Think they have no control over their circumstances	- Know they can always control how they respond to their circumstances
- Are problem-oriented	- Are solution-oriented

The key difference between the victor and the victim is that the victors take whatever life throws at them and they deal with it appropriately. The cards they're dealt do not hold them back or stop them from accomplishing their personal goals. The victims, on the other hand, allow the sporadic events that life throws at them to push them around and control their lives. The victim blames others as they hand over their personal power to things that are out of their control. As long as victims continue to point fingers, they will remain hostage to the unexpected incidences of life.

While reading "*The 5 a.m. Club*," by Robin Sharma, I read through a passage that I'd like to share because of the profound message it left in my mind and heart. Robin is describing a concept that he refers to as "Learned Victimhood."

> *"As we leave our youth, there's a pull toward complacency. We can start to coast, settle for what's familiar and lose the juicy desire to expand our frontiers. We adopt the paradigm of a victim. We make excuses and then recite them so many times we train our subconscious mind to think they are true. We blame other people and outer conditions for our struggles, and we condemn past events for our private wars. We grow cynical and lose the curiosity, wonder, compassion, and innocence we knew as kids. We become apathetic. Critical. Hardened. Mediocrity then becomes acceptable. And because this mindset is running within us each day, the viewpoint seems so very real to us. We truly believe that the story we are running reveals the truth—because we're so close to it. So, rather than showing leadership in our fields, owning our crafts by producing dazzling work and handcrafting delicious lives, we resign ourselves to average. But every time you become aware of yourself dropping into victim mode and make a more courageous choice, you rewrite the narrative. You raise your self-identity, elevate your self-respect and enrich your self-confidence. Each time you vote for your superior self you starve the weaker side and feed your inherent power. And as you do this with the consistency demanded by mastery, your ability to materialize whatever gifts you've been born with will only grow."*

This book is an absolute *must read*. The way Robin Sharma articulates his messages and provides inspiration to his readers through a story like no other, is truly amazing. You can find it on the **BTB Website**!

When we observe the mentality of the victors, we can see that they all view setbacks as an opportunity to come back and overcome. There is no amount of adversity that can stop the victors from working towards actualizing their vision because they know what they want, and they know they will get it so long as they persist. What happens *to* the victors doesn't matter in the end because the victors are not controlled by what happens *to* them. The victors know that they are in complete control of responding to these unforeseen and unexpected turbulences, and they work towards their goals in spite of their presence. They remain focused on taking themselves to the next level. Remember this: *nothing external can phase the internal*!

MY TRANSITION

When I reflect on my own life, it's crazy to look back on all of the things that have happened and believe that they all have a purpose! I actually believe that even the tough times I faced growing up have made me stronger and are the foundation of who I have become today. I know that life isn't always going to be fair. Things aren't always going to be perfect. That's just the way it is, isn't it? Unexpected adversities showcase themselves from time to time and we need to accept their reality as real. However, in the midst of the chaos, time will pass regardless because *life goes on with or without you*. The ones who succeed through the trials and unexpected bumps are the ones who remain resilient and assume responsibility for what happens next. They take control of the controllables, even in the midst of their trials!

The one and only thing that we as humans have in our complete control is how we decide to react and respond to our conditions. Point. Blank. Simple.

I've struggled with this concept a lot, especially as a young player growing up. When a coach didn't play me as much as I wanted, or if things weren't going my way on the field, I always wanted to look for someone or something else to blame. I was too scared to tuck my chin, swallow my pride, stand up for myself, and fight back. I never wanted to be the reason why things weren't going according to the plan. But after learning and adapting a new mind-set, I began to take matters in my own hands.

Focusing only on what I could do in tough situations, rather than complain about things I couldn't, has allowed me to progress into the person and player I am today. During one of my first years playing at the professional level, I faced an opportunity to showcase a victor's mindset. I was about to start preseason training and camp was just around the corner. I entered preseason as fit as I could be, stronger than most of the other guys on my team, and was expecting to have a breakout year. I had put in a lot of work in the offseason to ensure that this coming season was going to be my best one yet.

I started in the first game of the season that year, scored a goal, and won "man of the match" honors as we fought back hard after being down 2-0 at half. We ended up tying the game after a hard, demanding 90 minutes. Later the following week, in the buildup to our next game, I found out that I was being pulled out of the starting 11. I didn't understand why I was being pulled out and I was enraged. I didn't get it. What did I do? Was I not good enough? Did I make a mistake? I thought it was outrageous and you can imagine the whirlwind of negative thoughts that were shooting throughout my mind.

One of my teammates at the time, an older veteran player, could see my disappointment one day on the training pitch. He was one of the guys who I had looked up to most on my team and I thought it was a good time to get some advice. I asked him what he thought about the situation, after expressing sheer annoyance with the circumstances I was facing.

He told me a story about when he went to a National Team camp prior to a World Cup tournament a few years back. During this time, he was on a preliminary roster of 32 guys who all had a chance to play on the biggest soccer stage on the planet. He told me that while he was away at the camp, he called an old coach of his to get some advice because of the extreme nerves he was dealing with during the days leading up to the announcement of the roster cut. As you can imagine, those sorts of emotions can affect your performance if you allow them to and really dominate your mind. If you're bottled up by anxiety and nervousness, you might not play well enough during the trial week to make that final roster, so you need to be able to get your emotions and feelings in check.

So, after a bit of talking back and forth, he told me that he had asked his former coach what he thought he should do that might help him in this situation. His old manager responded by saying that he should focus on "controlling the things that he could control." That was exactly what he told me on that same day. My teammate proceeded by asking me, "what are the things that are in your control?"

I paused for a minute and looked at him, confused, because he wasn't giving me the answer I wanted to hear. After a few moments of awkward silence from me not knowing what to say, he answered for me by saying, "the only thing you can control is your attitude in training, your work ethic throughout the week, and how you actually perform with whatever minutes the coach does decide to give you. You can't control whether he is going to start you or even play you at all. The only thing you can focus on is making sure that if you do get a chance to step on the pitch, you make the most of it."

I remember thinking... "Unfortunately, he's right." Because I wanted to change the circumstances. I wanted to change the coach's mind. It took a little while for those words to sink in, mostly because my emotions were taking over my thoughts and I needed some time to let them calm down. I needed to level out my head. Over the course of the following week, I took my teammates advice to heart and brought his idea on board. Moving forward, that piece of advice has stuck with me throughout everything I've been through so far in my career.

When the next game rolled around, I put into practice the advice I'd received a week prior. I came on as a substitute in the following matches and completely turned the games around when I stepped onto the field. I came into one of the games when the score was 3-2, with probably around 20 to 30 minutes left. Within minutes of being on the field, I scored a goal to tie the game and the stadium erupted. The momentum was on our side and our team went on to win the match 4-3, catapulting us forward with what was a big win for us at that point of the season.

> ## "A man can fail many times, but he isn't a failure until he begins to blame someone else." —John Burroughs

What a moment and what a lesson I had learned that day. The reality was confirmed, and my beliefs were reassured with evidence that when you have a victor mindset and control the things you can, good things will come in time.

I could have very well victimized myself throughout the week leading up to that game and been showcasing my disappointment. I could have allowed my emotions to affect my work ethic, causing me to have a negative attitude towards my teammates, and ultimately leading me to feeling helpless and hopeless. If I didn't maintain a positive attitude and a strong work ethic throughout that week of training, maybe I wouldn't have been as ready to grab hold of the opportunity I was given to play on the weekend. Who knows? All I know is that obtaining a victor's mindset trumps the victim's mindset every day of the week! Even though this was a subtle example, I feel it's very powerful when talking about taking accountability for the situation you are in and doing all the things you can, within your control, to make sure you get your desired results in the future. Regardless of whether or not things are happening the way you like.

NECESSARY BUT NOT EASY

It's really hard not to make excuses and point fingers when things aren't panning out exactly how you'd imagined. Especially in more extreme cases where the situations are more dire. I'm not saying it's easy because, I personally, don't know what it's like to be in your situation and deal with whatever you're dealing with. But I do know that assuming full responsibility for your life and not making excuses is an instrumental part of the formula for success.

YOUR ACTION ITEM. Let's get real! Write down a few of excuses you have been making recently that aren't supporting your dream to live the life you desire.

1.

2.

3.

Now, analyze what you've written down and flip the script. Write down how you're going to use your circumstances to get stronger and move yourself forward.

1.

2.

3.

Good! Now you've completely changed the trajectory of your life because you're assuming full responsibility for it. I know it's much easier to play the victim and blame external things because then you don't have to go through the pain you know will come from facing your reality head on. It's hard to face those occurrences with courage because of the sadness and pain that comes along with going through it. That's called a *growing experience.* Because you know what else? This can work to your advantage because the world loves an underdog story. The world loves to see people beat the odds and overcome their harsh environments. The world favors those who crawl out of the trenches and defy their circumstances. Those who come from the bottom and change their lives for the better. You can do it. You can do whatever you put your mind to no matter where you're currently at in your life!

And a lot of the time our situations aren't as bad as we think. There are many other people out there who have it so much worse, unfortunately. By seeing how blessed we actually still are, in spite of our environments, helps limit our excuses. Just know that someone always has it worse than you do. *Always*. So be grateful for the situation you are in, even if it sucks right now. Even if it's hard, know that with all adversities comes the seed of opportunity to create something marvelous. Don't make excuses for yourself. Find your power within to dig yourself out of whatever hole you find yourself in. Know that there is someone out there who has faced tougher odds, more traumatic situations, etc., but has still found a way to climb out, often scratching and clawing for everything on their way towards the top of the mountain. The only difference is that they didn't make any excuses over the course of their lives.

The ones who experience great victory take matters into their own hands, and you can too! See it, believe it, achieve it! You can do it if you take full accountability for where you are right now. Be honest with yourself, even if it's hard. This will give you the assurance you need. Assuming full responsibility for your current reality gives you true power in knowing that you're in control of the outcomes of your life. Taking extreme ownership will force you to start taking action towards becoming the new version of yourself. The one that you've longed to become.

YOUR ACTION ITEM. Write down what is in your control, right now:

1.

2.

3.

Make a promise to yourself that you're going to cut out all excuses and make life happen for you, rather than letting it happen to you.

"If it's important you'll find a way, if not, you'll find an excuse." —Daniel Decker

You've now learned the majority of the principles that make up BTB. They encompass what BTB is all about. They support the BTB lifestyle. I've laid out how you need to strive to constantly learn from the best, how important it is to use your vision to fuel your drive, how to implement the three D's, followed by a series of tips on habits, confidence, and finding the source of power that lies in being driven by your fears. Now, I want to walk you through the single most important step when it comes to achieving success. *Execution*. That is where we are going next.

EXECUTING YOUR PLAN FOR SUCCESS

Success is the direct result of taking continued actions consistently, while making constant adjustments along the way. You live, you learn, you take action to implement the new things you learn. You make mistakes, you refine your strategy, and you take action. You must always continuously take action in order to achieve.

As you have gone over the tactics and principles laid out for you throughout this book, I surely hope that you've learned something. That you've gained some new knowledge on stuff you can do that has the potential to further improve the quality of your life. I hope you've gained knowledge that you can *use*. You're now up to full speed and are aware of some routines you can implement into your life that can bring you the everlasting success you desire. From here on out, it is up to *you*!

No amount of reading or learning is going to make your dreams come true on their own. It is your responsibility to act upon the things you're learning. Otherwise, what's the point? Not only does that include the information that you've gathered from this book, but from every other book you read as well. Every podcast, every article, whatever it may be. Not to mention your own personal experiences.

Making the decision to *act* will tie all of the components of BTB together. Learning from the best requires you to act by being intentional about learning and making sure you're personally growing every day. Whether that be physically picking up a book or pressing play on the podcast for your car ride to work. Make it happen!

Having a vision calls on you to *act* because you will need to actually take the time to sit with yourself and visualize the life you truly want. Having good habits mandates that you *act* upon your desires through daily discipline and dedication to the process. Every step necessitates *action*. Without action we have nothing. Your map has been created, your goals have been identified, and now it is time to execute.

GO. ALL. IN.

In order to execute your plan for success, you can't be half in, half out. You can't only be committed to becoming the best version of yourself only half of the time. Aspiring to reach your maximum potential requires that you go all in. It demands that you *Bet On Yourself* today, tomorrow, and every day from here on out. No more half in, half out. It's time to go all in!

"Yeah, I like coffee. But nothing I do is half and half." —Chris Mueller

You would be doing yourself a true injustice by not executing your plan for success. You owe it to yourself to take a leap of faith. Reading books and absorbing a stupendous amount of material, gaining precious knowledge, but not backing it up isn't fair to those who don't have the same level of awareness as you. You would only be fooling yourself because you have the knowledge and awareness in the first place. You know what is required. Simply not following through seems wrong!

Execution is taking matters into your own hands. Nothing is going to be given to you! Everything I talk about when it comes to having a motivating vision, making sacrifice, confidence, or good habits, none of it is going to help you make a difference in your own life unless you are deliberate about applying what you have learned into your everyday life. You need to go out and take action.

I know how obvious this sounds. I'm not oblivious to that. However, I do know from my own experiences, how easy it can be to just skim through a book without taking any further steps because reading in itself makes you feel like you are doing something worthwhile. Feeding your mind with a repeatedly positive, inspiring message won't do any harm. Reading and absorbing empowering material will help you if you decide to act or not. But the degree to which you'll see the effects in your life will be multiplied if you do act on them. Although you will feel like you are making loads of progress—and you are by picking up a book in the first place—going through the information will improve the quality of your thoughts, but by itself will not drastically change life. Only you have the power to do that.

The knowledge you get from reading books is great. I have mentioned many times throughout this book how reading one book changed my life. However, reading it wasn't actually what altered my reality; it was my decision to execute the principles I learned while reading! I was intentional about practicing the lessons I learned in the book. That willingness to act is what has brought me to where I am today.

> **"The willingness to do whatever it takes,
> to act in spite of fear,
> is the basis of courage."** —Michael Hyatt

Use the information you have acquired to drive you and take the steps necessary to complete the mission you started. It's on you. Nobody else can hold that responsibility for you. Your internal drive needs to be an unbreakable force field that won't allow anything external throw you off course. You need to keep your focus aligned with what you deeply desire and do everything in your control to make sure it happens. Because you're going to be tested in a variety of ways along your path. If you aren't being tested, you aren't doing anything challenging enough to stretch your potential, allowing you to become the best you can be.

How badly do you want to be successful? What are you willing to sacrifice? What are you willing to do? How far are you willing to go to get the things you want? You won't make the most out of your life unless you are willing to take action yourself and apply the things you learn to your process. Maximize your time and improve your efficiency. Fill the time blocks of your day-to-day planner with actions or experiences that will empower and provide you with a positive feeling about the things that you're doing.

NO HESITATION

Talking and reading about having big dreams is one thing. Hearing inspirational stories of people who have started from the bottom and made it through hell to get the glory they utterly desired can be moving. When it comes down to it, your future is in your own hands. It's up to you to get the job done. The information and resources that we have today is all accessible to you and me, right now. It's literally at our fingertips through our smartphones! All it takes? A bit of courage for you to take that first step! Because in my opinion, the hardest thing is starting. It's tempting to say things like:

- *"I'll start tomorrow."*
- *"I've got time."*
- *"There's no rush."*

Nothing urges me more! *Why wait*? Tomorrow isn't promised! Take action now and begin to build the foundation for accomplishing the things that you are wholly craving. Reading about successful individuals who seem like they're gifted a superpower that has propelled them to unbelievable levels of fame or fortune is knowledge. But from what we have learned, knowledge is not power. It's only potential power.

> **"Inaction breeds doubt and fear. Action breeds confidence and courage. If you want to conquer fear, don't sit at home and think about it. Go out and get busy."** —Dale Carnegie

Everyone who has accomplished the greatest tasks throughout our lives are regular people, just like you and me! The *only* difference lies in their determination, how far they were able to see beyond their current circumstances to push the limits and live out their dreams in a fulfilling future. They were able to push further when everyone else had enough. They prepared themselves down to the finest detail so that when their opportunity came to attack and pounce, they were ready, and they took full advantage of it. They executed. They acted on their game plan. They *made it happen.*

I remember reading about Mark Cubans come up in his book "*How to Win at the Sport of Business.*" He talked about how when he finally caught his break in business and started to see some success, people called him lucky. However, what not many people know is that he was sleeping on couches, grinding hard every single day, reading computer manuals in his free time. You make your own luck.

"Success is what you do before and after you do everything you're supposed to." —Grant Cardone

Just like Mark, you have to go out and do it for yourself. Act! Be a beast in your field. Don't take no for an answer. Find a way. Don't let anyone tell you that you can't do something. You can do anything you want, and you can be anything you want with the right mindset.

The execution phase includes everything from the small details, to the overlying strategy, to all of the extra work that lies ahead. Everyone—and I mean *everyone*—does what they are *supposed* to do. If you take that route, you're on your way to becoming mediocre. Doing just what you're supposed to do will just ensure that you are like everyone else.

What are we striving for here? What are *you* striving for? To be like everyone else? To fit in? Or to be the best? To be the best version of yourself? To defy the odds and to maximize your potential? Then you *must* do more than is required from you. The extra hours, the extra work, the additional purposeful steps you take towards becoming the person you want to be is what will separate you from the rest. You cannot get there by being like everyone else and settling for doing what you're supposed to. Go above and beyond and take your dedication to the next level by constantly executing your strategy towards becoming *the best*.

I came across this quote from Thomas Edison and it struck me because of how sadly true it is...

"Opportunity is missed by most people because it is dressed in overalls and looks like work." —Thomas Edison

What a wonderful statement... but kind of unfortunate, don't you think? Too many individuals know what it takes to be successful, but they also know that it takes a lot of hard work, and they are intimidated by that. They know it will not be easy to accomplish anything worthwhile. There are never guarantees at the end of any road, so why try anyways? Tomorrow isn't guaranteed but you expect your success to be. How does that make sense?

Realize that whatever it is you are setting out to do is going to demand a great deal of execution. You're going to have to act and actually use your expertise to create the life you desire.

THE PRESEASON GRIND

Any professional athlete will tell you that preseason training is one of the most difficult periods of the year. It's extremely demanding and is a blocked-out time frame meant to get you into optimal physical and mental shape for the duration of the regular and post seasons. There was a year in my career where my team and I went to Cancun in Mexico for a training camp. I had been waking up at 5:30 a.m. to get in my daily reading and quiet time to settle and prepare my mind for the day. I always do this process before training in my normal daily routine, so I had to make sure I made the time to continue the habit.

This time was insanely busy and chaotic! After finishing my reading, the first training session at 7:30 a.m. We had to ride our bikes a mile-and-a-half to the field to practice and train for an hour and a half or so, followed by another mile-and-a-half bike ride back. At 10 a.m. we were gifted with our first meal of the day, breakfast! That was the time to refuel and revamp for what was to come. After breakfast we had our next session at noon out on the beach. By this point, it's the middle of the day, and we're doing sand sprints, weighted squats, vertical squat jumps, upper body training, and many other work sequences intended to build strength. The treatment and recovery process began after lunch to ensure our bodies were ready for our third training session of the day, which would always hang over our heads. For the night session, it's back out to the field. Including the mile-and-a-half bike ride to and from. Long days doesn't even begin to describe it!

You get the point. It's a lot of work that includes three training sessions per day. Everyone is tired, sore, beat, and waiting for this camp to end so we can get back home and start the regular season. With a small increment of time in between my first and second practice times, it sounded heavenly to take a nap for 30 minutes, or to put my head down and just relax a little. Instead, I chose to be out there on my balcony, writing *this* book, telling you guys about how important it is to put in the work! When you have a "why" that's strong enough and your desires run deep enough, you'll always find a way. Revert back to your "why," as Simon Sinek constantly refers to, and as I touched on in earlier chapters:

> *To inspire anyone and everyone to fearlessly aspire to be great. To show people that through commitment, consistency, hard work, sacrifice, and discipline that anything is possible. Dream big and act today towards what you want tomorrow. Be the Best. #BTB*

A "why" so powerful that it pushes me to continue to work, to train, to watch, to recover, to read, to write, to push myself beyond the limits to provide people with a credible reference whom they can look to during tough times of their own. Because even though I don't really feel like writing in this very moment, I know that if I don't get to it now, I won't get to it today, which won't help me accomplish my long-term goals either. Staying focused on trying to *win the day*, beating resistance on a day-to-day basis, will provide me with the momentum I need to string the many wins together required to create the success I desire.

Do you see where I am going with this? I feel like people nowadays are daunted by the work it will take to do something great, and it's hard for me to grasp why. The fulfillment of accomplishing something that you know you busted your ass for is the best feeling in the world! It will alter your identity and your belief. It will empower you and give undeniable confidence in yourself that you can do anything you put your mind to. I cannot emphasize enough the importance of implementing all of the knowledge you have gained along the way to get to where you're going. Everything you have ever wanted is out there for the taking. But it really doesn't matter if I tell you a million times to act and to execute if you don't really believe you can. Your limiting beliefs aren't going to motivate you to take action right now.

> ## "To me, ideas are worth nothing unless executed.
> ## They are just a multiplier.
> ## Execution is worth millions." —Steve Jobs

Action and execution are the most important pieces of the puzzle, because without them, you are going to be the same person 10 years from now as you are today. You're off to a great start by picking up this book and choosing to read it in the first place. You're actually way ahead of the pack already! These actions are going to help you become the person you want to be!

Start now and do something today that you will be thankful for tomorrow. Choose to take action and do something extra that will soon help you in reaching your goals. Make them clear and create a map as to what you need to do to get there.

YOUR ACTION ITEM. Pause from the reading for a second and write down something right now that you want to change about your life. Next, create a plan as to how you are going to do it! Take a minute and start to brainstorm. Put the pen to paper and write out three new ways you can take action in order to execute the plan you've created to achieve your goals:

1.

2.

3.

GET DESPERATE...

After we had just finished near last place in the Big Ten Conference, if I told you that the following year, we would be the top contenders for the title and make it to the championship games, you would have told me I was crazy. After my freshman year of college, if I told you that I believed I could help my team win its first outright Big Ten Championship in school history, you would have looked at me like I was from a different planet. Of course, there are going to be people who think it never could happen. The easy thing to do would have been to come up with a load of excuses as to why reaching for something like that, at that time, was simply a waste of time. Why put in the work to try and be the best when there are teams like Indiana, Maryland, and Michigan State who are constantly bringing in the top recruits and contending for the title? I had a million reasons backing the belief that what I wanted couldn't happen. That there was no reason to create a plan, no reason to act, and no reason to execute.

"Desperation breeds a beast." —Russ

Looking back now I realize that the phase of my life when I was playing college soccer, in the Big Ten, was such a small endeavor in the grand picture of the football world. When I tell my current teammates in the pros about my time at Wisconsin and about playing college soccer in the Big Ten, over half of them have no idea what that even is. As I sit in deep reflection, it was such an important piece of my past because of the fuel, growth, and awareness it provided me with. I was able to see the direct results I received from the work I had been putting in for years prior! That lesson literally *changed me.*

Winning that trophy and being the best team in the Big Ten looked like an impossible task at the time. It looked like we were about to attempt hiking up Mount Everest but starting underground! After going into college as not being a top recruit, not getting as much scholarship money as many of the other guys in my class, I was not supposed to turn out as one of the best players on my team from the beginning. Starting my first two years in college ball as a bench/role player, I had two seasons left. If I told you I was going to become the *only* two-time All-American in Wisconsin soccer history, that was a dream that seemed highly improbable. Certainly, it would have been impossible if I was to just sit around and hope for it to happen. Especially when there were no guarantees. I didn't know that all of the work and the sacrifices I was going to make would lead me to where I am today! But I did it anyway. I believed. Sure, the odds were against me. But with a relentless determination, a massive amount of action, and a huge amount of work, I was able to accomplish everything I wanted at that time and more.

I have only gained more awareness about myself and learned from so many other new experiences along the way. Now I have more drive than ever to go and get what I want out of my own life and my career. I was desperate for success. I was desperate to be the best I could be. I was desperate to help my team win. For that reason, because I was desperate for more, I was able to take an insane amount of action that propelled me towards accomplishing my goals. All of those late nights, early mornings, extra running, the extra weight sessions, the reading, the writing, stretching, and sacrificing, it all paid off in due time because now I am living out my dream. And the best part is that I'm only getting started...

My main goal, from the get-go of writing this book, has been to inspire kids of all ages and people from all around the world who come from a random place and want to become more, to live out their dreams, big or small, but don't necessarily see an out or aren't sure what to do. Even if I only sold 10 copies and influenced one person to go out and dare to be great, that would be enough for me. I want to encourage people to follow their dreams because I've seen how through hard work, anything is possible.

I want you to believe me when I say I have seen this process give back in my own life in so many aspects. I am so grateful that I gained this awareness when I was younger. I am so thankful that I stuck to the process I created. I am so grateful that God allowed me to succeed and prove these principles correct. I want us to continue to push on together and defy the limitations that society has set on us as individuals. We are all made for more!

SACRIFICE

Sacrifice is defined as *"the act of giving up something valued for the sake of something else regarded as more important or worthy."* Giving something up valued for the sake of something else. Not just anything else... something more *important* and *worthy*.

Now before moving on, let me ask you a question. What is more valuable than yourself? What is more worthy than committing yourself to excellence and striving to become something more? What is more valuable than the investment in yourself? Sacrifice is mandatory!

I feel like sacrifice is disregarded in many success stories because it is a hard topic to talk about. Not too many individuals want to know that in order to gain ground in one area, they will have to give up something else that's important to them. Unfortunately, many individuals talk about the things they want and the things they desire, although they don't always back up what they say with their actions.

A principle that will become clear, as you continue to pull ahead of the pack, in this metaphorical race towards the top is that the small details in-between make the difference between who wins and who loses. People who give up many things in order to give themselves that personal edge is what ultimately will bring them victory. This is no easy feat. It's one thing to say, and it is another thing to do. It's not easy to sacrifice things that have now become social norms in our lives in order to take that competitive advantage. If you want to be a top professional athlete, a top businessperson, or first in your class at your school, you are going to have to give up in some aspects of your life to accomplish such a goal. These sacrifices usually include things like time with your family and friends, your social life, and sleep.

I remember when I was much younger, my best friend at the time and I were obsessed with the idea and the possibility of becoming professional soccer players. There were so many days and nights that we would go to a field near our houses after training to practice for hours on our own, envisioning what it would feel like to score a goal in a stadium in front of thousands of people. Feeling that adrenaline rush would push us to constantly make sacrifices in order to make that feeling a reality. Literally, when we'd be training out on the field long after the sun had set, we'd shoot a ton of balls and if they hit the back of the net, we'd run off to the corner of the field celebrating like we'd just scored the winning goal in the World Cup final! It was the best feeling ever and something I longed to feel in real life. I didn't want to only imagine it, though, I wanted to *live it*. And in order to give ourselves the best possible chance at doing so, we had to step away and disengage from a lot of the activities that the majority of other kids our age were doing.

> ### "As soon as you want to succeed as bad as you want to breathe, then you'll be successful."
> —Eric Thomas

Let that sink in. As soon as you want to succeed as bad as you want to breathe, then you'll be successful. It couldn't be put into simpler terms. Think of an instance where you've heard people talk about something they want, something they want to do, somewhere they want to go. People talk the talk, all while they're engaging in activities that contradict exactly what they just said they wanted to do. When I heard that phrase for the first time it lit a fire in my heart because it represented sacrifice. In order to experience something that very few people have the opportunity to, you have to be willing to sacrifice more than most people are. It's a part of the process and is a prerequisite for success.

As a young kid with huge aspirations, when I came to understand that some of my actions were not completely aligned with my vision, I felt a wave of guilt. It was a harsh moment but an important realization me. A wakeup call, if you will. How could I, as a 16-year-old kid, be going around telling people that I wanted to play soccer professionally, all while I was out hanging out with the wrong crowds and doing the wrong things. Partaking in activities that weren't going to help make my dreams come true? I was aspiring to play professional soccer. That's no easy feat. But because I was out hanging out with people for the sole purpose of trying to look cool, fit in, and get with the norm, it made me a bit of a hypocrite. Sadly, that's the brutal, honest truth. I didn't have the right to truthfully say at the time that I wanted my dream bad enough because I wasn't being a man of my word and backing up my talk with legitimate action.

> **"Character cannot be developed in the ease and quiet.**
> **Only through the experience of trial and suffering can**
> **the soul be strengthened, vision cleared, ambition inspired,**
> **and success achieved."** —Helen Keller

The idea revolving around sacrifice made me feel a pain, deep in my core foundation, because I value authenticity and being a man of my word. What I realized was that I wasn't doing that, and it was attacking my values. My sense of worth, being someone who always backed the talk, wasn't quite the case back then.

The message above has stuck with me through thick and thin up until this very moment. These are the types of things you need to be sacrificing to get what you really want. You need to be willing to sacrifice a night out with your friends in order to stay in and take care of yourself. You need to be hungry enough to get out of bed and get an extra workout in the gym before training. You need to want to succeed bad enough that you get to the office before everyone else, put in a day full of work, and then be the last one to leave.

YOUR DAILY EQUATION

Work + Learning + Extra Work = (24 Hours of the day) = Leisure Time + Social Life + Sleep

Look at this standard equation. *Sacrifice* in your life works similarly to this simple mathematic equation. As one side of the equation goes up, by making additions, the other side must come down, by making some subtractions. If you are to increase the amount of time you're learning about your craft, making adjustments working on yourself, and practicing self-mastery, you're consequentially going to have to *sacrifice* time with your friends, nights out on the weekend, or that extra hour of sleep. This game is all about sacrifice. What are you willing to give up in order to get and experience the things you desire? That's something you're going to have to answer for yourself, but I'm telling you that once you eliminate what doesn't really matter, you're going to feel a whole lot better about what you're doing and where you're going.

DELAYED GRATIFICATION > INSTANT GRATIFICATION

As you begin to sacrifice the things you feel necessary in order to reach your goal, expect it to be hard in the beginning. Saying "no" to your friends the first couple of times when they're all going out and having a good ol' time while you're stuck at home, by yourself, watching film or doing whatever it is you have to do, is going to be tough initially. For real. It is. I've been there and felt that loneliness. But I promise you, the delayed gratification will be much stronger than that instant and momentary gratification!

You will have plenty of people who are going to want to be your friend when you get to where you want to go. The route to grand success and personal accomplishment will be lonely. That's just how it is. No one's going to be there with you, cheering you on while you're doing the extra work. You got to do that all yourself. The ones who are willing to give up everything for their dreams are a rare breed. The ones who are authentic about what they want and not concerned with intangibles that have no value in assisting them in getting where they want to go are a rare breed. Those who strive to be the best under all circumstances, the ones who have that fire inside that surpasses all of the external components, who are driven by something deeper are a rare breed. Be willing to make a bigger sacrifice for the greater good. Starve yourself of the instant gratification you long for and commit yourself to the delayed gratification that will come from making the sacrifices necessary to succeed. Make a promise to chase down the things you utterly desire with a true conviction. Construct the willingness to give up whatever stands in the way of reaching your goals.

"It's lonely at the top. That's why a Ferrari has two seats, and a bus has 50." —SelfMotivateOfficial

Execute your game plan. BTB is about creating a lifestyle for yourself that will increase that likelihood of bringing success, happiness, and joy to you and your family. It's about working hard but also not losing track of the moment. Thus far in the book, we have covered the many principles of the

BTB process. The future-oriented focus that encompasses your goals and forces you to think about where you're trying to go.

For the last few sections of the book, I want to provide you with some tips and advice on how to cultivate joy in the present, in spite of your focus on what is yet to come. Some extremely helpful points for staying and being positive, having an attitude of gratitude, and finding the balance, all lie in the final pages ahead. By shifting our focus to improving our ability to be present in this moment, in the here and now, will in turn, allow you to win each and every day. That power of supreme presence will ultimately allow you to realize everything you desire. I hope you've enjoyed what you've learned up until now. Let's keep going!

PRACTICE
GRATITUDE AND
A POSITIVE
ATTITUDE

Be present. Be here. Be exactly where your feet are. Be open and try to learn these lessons with the best of your ability. Try not to worry about what you have to do later, what obligations you have throughout your day, or how many meetings you have on your schedule. Right now, you're sitting with a book in hand and enjoying your time. You have nothing else to do other than read your book and appreciate this very moment. Now let's move forward...

POSITIVE ATTITUDE

The life we are living is a beautiful one. It is precious and unique. No two people share the same experiences and paradigms. Each life is lived solely on its own, and the freedom to choose how to live and think is in control of the individual.

I believe a quality that is extremely undervalued in our world is the ability to maintain a positive attitude. From my perspective, individuals who have been able to keep their thoughts optimistic, regardless of what was happening around them, seem to be the more successful and happier people. I want to give you my two cents on why I think this characteristic is such an important feature for those on a mission to fulfill their vision. If we are able to take a step back in order to understand how fragile and how wonderful this life really is, it would allow us the ability to see the bigger picture. The practice of opening yourself up to seeing things as they are, with no attachments, can provide you with the clarity and peace you need during testing times.

Since I have become more aware of the power that your attitude has on the quality of your life, I felt compelled to share my findings. Happiness is an internal state that can only be sought for with intention by the individual. Practicing gratitude supports a positive attitude and optimistic outlook. Having an attitude of gratitude is the spark to the fire and can immediately help you change the way you view what happens around you. The uncanny ability to see the bright side in all situations. We should try to flip what happens *to* us into something that happens *for* us. The decision is *ours*... and I want to help you discover how to make that choice. The choice that will be a life of fulfillment, a life of abundance, and a life of happiness. The power to choose, the power that already lies inside of you, is just a few pages away!

> **"If you are depressed, you are living in the past.**
> **If you are anxious, you are living in the future.**
> **If you are at peace, you are living in the present."** —Lao Tzu

Maintaining a positive attitude and being optimistic when life isn't going your way is imperative for your mental health as you continue your journey towards success. We continuously face challenges on a day-to-day basis that vary in size and relevance. When these tests of life come to the surface, I see them as an opportunity for all of us to practice our mental toughness. What do I mean by mental toughness? I mean that when something in your life happens to you, you're able to categorize these events as *external*. That is because they are out of your range of control. The external cannot phase the *internal*. What you do have control over? You have the power to choose your thoughts, internally, while everything may be breaking down around you, externally.

Maintaining a positive attitude will show you the degree to which you are mentally tough and able to subside the challenges that life has to offer. When life takes a twist or a turn and we hit a bump in the road, it's natural to have pessimistic thoughts and feelings of fear take over our minds, causing us to victimize ourselves. The importance of fighting off that wave of negativity from the get-go will be a substantial component to your general health and happiness. A principle that is easy to talk about but extremely difficult to put into practice.

I can't overestimate the importance of having a positive attitude and a clear mindset throughout the trials and tribulations you'll face on your journey through BTB. I haven't met one person or read any stories about anyone who lived through a compelling journey toward achieving their idea of success and had only experienced the peaks along the way. Peaks without the valleys only happens in fairytales. Everyone, and I mean *everyone*, encounters obstacles throughout their journey, and everyone will fail at one time or another. Don't for even a second think that you're the only one who has to put up with the unexpected obstacles that life throws at us! As a matter of fact, you should expect them. Strive to challenge yourself by putting yourself in situations where failure is possible.

"Success is going from failure to failure without loss of enthusiasm." —Winston Churchill

The only difference between someone who is successful and someone who is not lies in the way they handle these minor setbacks. Let us begin to change the way we see them. View them in a positive frame of mind rather than a negative one.

Easier said than done—especially when you are in the midst of a tough time or a rigid stretch. Don't get down on yourself. Don't lose your faith in the process when things aren't going as well as you maybe had previously planned. Understand the reality that everyone goes through rough patches and that you're not the first one to encounter a mishap. The ones who make it through the storms are simply strong enough, mentally, to be able to persist in spite of the bad weather. They don't quit and they never give up.

You must maintain a positive attitude throughout your journey, because if you don't look at every loss you take as a lesson and as an opportunity to learn, it will cost you in the long run. Being overly optimistic about the circumstances you come across will enhance your self-belief and convince you that you have what it takes to make it through whatever setbacks you face.

Have you ever tried to keep track of how productive you were on a day that you spent upset, disappointed, down on yourself, or with a negative attitude? I know I have and every time I catch myself in that sort of state, it feels like a day that is completely wasted. Not only in terms of productivity either, but in the sense that life happens and goes by so fast. Why should we waste any time in a negative state of mind if the way we decide to think is a choice!

"The only time we waste is the time we spend in a negative state."
—Chris Mueller

If you are not operating throughout your daily routines with a positive attitude and with a clear mind, you are inevitably putting yourself at a disadvantage. Each and every day that we're blessed to experience is independent and has its own unique lessons and experiences waiting for you. Life is a beautiful mystery and it's a conscious decision that you can make to see it that way!

Shifting your perception of negative, external events as situations that are teaching you something is instrumental to your levels of happiness and joy. Failures are not defining moments. Far too often we see people identify themselves as their failures because things didn't happen the way they thought they should have originally. We are too easily discouraged. Don't attach more meaning to the failures and setbacks you experience than is necessary to learn and move on. Don't lose confidence in yourself and in your abilities. There's no need to get down on yourself, so don't!

Don't attach any meaning to your failures. That will only bring you negative energy, and that's what we are trying to stay away from. Negative energy is toxic. Negative energy is poison that has the potential to sabotage your mission. Negative energy is draining. When you are experiencing its effects, you can feel the toll it takes on your body and on your well-being. Radiating positive vibes and good energy, while keeping your mind-frame free from pessimistic thoughts, will be a determining factor not only to your success and whether or not you achieve your goals, but to your personal health and well-being as well.

> **"Train your mind to see the good in everything.
> Positivity is a choice. The happiness of your life depends
> on the quality of your thoughts."** —Marcus Aurelius

We have the power to choose. Do you want to choose to live in a positive state of mind or a negative one? When you are in a positive state of mind, don't you feel as if you overall level of happiness and contentment with your life is higher? If those thoughts and feelings are our own choices, why don't we choose to live that way all the time? We are the governors and directors of our thoughts and we get to choose how we perceive things. Why not see them in a positive fashion? A practice that won't only help you be successful in your occupation, but more importantly, should vastly improve the quality of your life!

Do your best not to give the power to anything external. Don't allow your happiness and contentment to be dependent on things always going your way. Whether or not there is traffic on your way to work, or a long line at Starbucks, whatever it may be, chose to be happy! Your happiness is only contingent on the manner that which you chose to think of and perceive the events that happen in your life. The power is yours and yours alone.

YOUR ACTION ITEM. Is there anything you can think of that you're experiencing right now that you've been viewing with a negative outlook? With a pessimistic frame of mind? I want to give you the opportunity to call it out and change the way you think about it. Take the wheel. You deserve to be happy and joyful in this very moment. Point out what might be holding you back and let's work on changing the way you think about it!

Something that has been robbing me of my joy is:

I'm going to choose to view it this way, from this day forward:

Seeing difficult situations from this perspective will allow you to maintain a positive attitude along the ups and downs that life brings. Facing failure is inevitable. You will experience challenges in some way, shape, or form at some point in your life! Once you adapt that mindfulness and awareness, once you choose to perceive your circumstances from a positive point of view, you have ultimately gained the true wealth that everyone is searching for in this life. The ability to be *happy* in spite of the external situations that are occurring around you. When you are in a positive state of mind, you will be able to think clearer, be happier, and find more joy as you go throughout your daily life. Make that choice, *now*!

You may be asking and thinking... "I know I'm supposed to be positive, but I just don't really know how." Or, "I know how important having a positive attitude is, but I can't seem to grasp its fullness." That's where an attitude of gratitude can help kick start the process. A positive outlook can be ignited by practicing gratitude.

ATTITUDE OF GRATITUDE

Your number one priority from here on out that will enhance every aspect of your life should be to adapt an attitude of gratitude. Being grateful for everything you have—and when I say everything, I mean *everything*—

will be a true difference maker in improving the eminence of your life! Maintaining a positive attitude can be enriched by adapting the practice of learning how to be grateful. Let's talk some more about the power that lies behind the daily practice of expressing gratitude.

Fill your heart and focus your mind on everything in your life that you're grateful for. Where your focus goes, energy flows! If you consistently focus on things that make you upset or leave you feeling frustrated, it will stir up disempowering emotions that will take over your mind and body. Ultimately destroying your productivity and efficiency because of the mood you've created which won't help you accomplish the things you want! When you focus primarily on how blessed you are and how amazing your life really is, you can take a step back and breathe a breath of fresh air. You can feel gratitude for things being the way that they are.

"The more thankful I became, the more my bounty increased. That's because—for sure—what you focus on expands. When you focus on the goodness in life, you create more of it." —Oprah Winfrey

Feel that intense sense of thankfulness for all that you have and for all of the people around you. By adopting an attitude of gratitude, you are destined to end up in a more conscious, aware, and positive state *consistently*.

In *"Awaken The Giant Within,"* Tony Robbins talks about how we should learn to really *feel* our disempowering emotions along with our empowering ones. This includes the feelings of uncertainty, guilt, resentment, disappointment, anxiety, and fear, among other negative feelings. We must learn to see and be grateful for the signals coming from our bodies and that includes all of our feelings and every one of our sensations. What this means is that our minds and bodies are sending us a message. That message is saying that a *change* needs to be made. Somewhere, for some reason, we are not being fulfilled in that specific moment, and it's causing us to feel down or negative. Our brain releases signals of disempowerment to the rest of the body, which affects the way we think and the way we live our lives. In reality, we need to comprehend how a shift in our focus can literally change our lives instantaneously.

An example of this concept could be if you were to feel a wave of anxiety take over your body in a given situation. When you feel that emotion surface, why are you feeling that way? Your body is sending you the signal "*a change is required*" because anxiety stems from uncertainty and fear.

For me, I have these feelings at times before games. Sometimes I'm about to walk into a stadium full of tens of thousands of people who are there to watch me and my team perform. In this instance, I could be feeling anxiety because of the uncertainty of how things might play out. *Will we win the game? Will I play well? Will I score?* All of these thoughts can take over my mind and body. The emotions can be overwhelming if I give them the power to alter my state. That anxiety can paralyze my positive beliefs and shoot me down a spiral of negative emotions and thoughts. But after receiving the signal from my body and mind, that is when it becomes vital that I make the change that is required.

I realign myself through my breath. Adapt the attitude of gratitude for being able to do what I love, to be playing in stadiums full of thousands of people, and on having the opportunity to showcase my talents and personality through the game I'm about to play. I anchor in on having a positive attitude and being optimistic about the situation at hand. I remind myself that I am prepared for the challenges that lie ahead and I will face them with the belief that I can persevere! All of a sudden, I've taken the message that was sent from my body and I've managed my anxiety through my attitude of gratitude and my positive mindset. I'll step out onto the pitch and play the game to the best of my ability with complete confidence. I'll be *fearless*. I'll be ready to BTB!

Make the decision to see your disempowering emotions as action signals to step forward and make a change! Turn the negative into a positive. Use your ability to choose your thoughts, because that key decision to be

happy with your own life, in this very moment, can be made in an instant…
right now. It's your decision.

YOUR ACTION ITEM. Write down three action signals that you feel on a regular basis and brainstorm how you can manage those emotions when they come to the surface. Whether that be anxiety, sadness, fear, or whatever it is, put pen to paper and lay out some of the possibilities as to how you can recenter yourself. How you can make the decision to choose your thoughts in those moments. Use the messages as calls to action and start the process of change!

1.

2.

3.

FIND YOUR ANCHOR

I say this from my personal experience of having lived my life both ways—both pessimistic and optimistic, grateful and selfish. Once I adapted the mindset of being grateful for everything I had and for whatever happened in my life, no matter the situation, my level of contentment and overall happiness skyrocketed. I now believe that life happens *for* us, not *to* us. Because of that gained awareness, I try not to waste any of my precious days in a negative frame of mind.

Have you ever noticed that on those days when things aren't going your way and you feel down in the dumps or upset, you just don't feel up to take on the day with tenacity? Those days are extremely hard to push through and they make your day-to-day life so dull. Living in that frame of mind is a prison cell where you are controlled by your emotions and by external circumstances. I try and avoid those attitudes at all costs, but I am not perfect either. If I am ever feeling troubled with a present situation, frustrated about the past, or anxious about the future, a wave of uncertainty and fear can creep into my mind. It's times like these where overthinking and over processing my emotions becomes an enticing trap to fall into. These are the days I put too much focus on the things that are out of my control. That, consequently, won't help me accomplish my long-term goals.

It's during times like these where it's absolutely crucial to *find your anchor.* Finding a way to return to your foundation becomes increasingly important as you continue to climb the ladder of success towards your goals. Your anchor, an exercise that brings you relief from disempowering emotions, could be a couple of things. It could be taking a few long inhales and exhales where you use your breath to bring you back to the moment. It could be visualizing being in your safe place in order to bring yourself calmness and clarity. There are many ways you can release the negative thoughts bouncing around in your mind. Personally, I use my breath to re-center and realign with the present moment.

In his book *"Innercise,"* John Assarf talks about the power that taking a few deep breaths has on your subconscious mind, heart, and body. He talks about how anchoring in on your breath clears your focus and allows you to regain balance. I would highly recommend his book, it's seriously eye-opening and changed my perspective for the better! You can find it on the **BTB Website**.

Your anchor should be something that brings you back to reality and quiets your conscious mind that is full of worry, anxiety, and fear. Using your anchor should bring you back to a place of peace and solitude. Your anchor should be an exercise that brings you back to reality. Your anchor should assist in reminding you of all the amazing little things that are happening in your life. All of the little things you have to be grateful for.

THE LITTLE THINGS MATTER

As a lot of people who have gotten to know me a bit better over the past couple of years, know that something I love to do is *radiate positive energy.* I want everyone to feel the happiness I feel for being alive today. I want everyone to feel the gratitude I practice for solely existing in this moment, as much as I do! People tend to get curious about how I can go about my days in such a positive fashion. My answer is simple, it's because I don't overlook how blessed I am for *all of the little things* I have in my life.

Start to see the things you look past and take for granted every day as a true blessing. Something as simple as opening your eyes in the morning. Some people didn't wake up today. That's the truth! Don't take that privilege as anything other than a blessing. God, the Universe, a higher power, or whoever it is that you believe in, decided to grant you with another day of life. That's what it is! There are people out there who didn't get that same blessing today. Really. I know it's hard to see it that way and it's a saddening to think about … but it's true. If you have two legs and are able to walk, be grateful for that… because that also, is a blessing.

Sometimes when I am not feeling up for training, feeling tired, sore, fatigued, or whatever, I revert my focus to practicing gratitude. I'm thankful I even have the ability to go run, let alone play the game I love. I'll be walking out onto the training field at times and just take a moment to look at the clouds passing by the warm sun beating down on me, and the fact that I'm lacing up my cleats to "go to work." Best to cherish my situation and not take it for granted!

These are the little, subtle things I am talking about. Once you are able to adapt an attitude of gratitude for the stuff that you usually take for granted, watch your entire world change. You'll see how big of a difference it will make and how big of an impact it will have on your life. After you start to understand how amazing your life actually probably is, it will give you the unlimited power to embrace each and every single day and make the most out of the opportunity to improve your life.

This mindset will assist you in living the lifestyle that is the very title of this book, being the best version of yourself. You'll be astonished by how once you make this change it will start to change your perspective. Your positivity and thankfulness will bleed into the people around you. All because you've increased your level of gratitude, which will consequentially also increase your level of happiness.

Being grateful allows you to cultivate joy in the present moment and propels you not to live a life where you're constantly wishing for things to be different. That mindset will bring you nothing but disappointment. So, try and foster an attitude of gratitude and you will unconsciously be making the world a much better place because you've taken the initiative to see things differently yourself. You can't help anyone else if you don't help yourself first! Spread the good news, spread the love, spread the gratitude to your friends and family. Let them know that the choice to be happy and grateful for everything they have in their lives can be made right now!

YOUR ACTION ITEM. Write down ten little things that you have taken for granted recently but have chosen to now see as a blessing. I recommend doing this practice to start your day **every morning**. This practice puts those things in the forefront of your mind and will help you start your day off on the right foot. For now, let's start with ten...

1.

2.

3.

4.

5.

6.

7.

8.

9.

10.

An attitude of gratitude is what will push you to new levels. Being grateful will encourage your positive attitude and nourish you to fulfill your destiny!

Get your train of thought on the right track. Get yourself into a positive state of mind. It will allow you to feel ready to tackle your day with a fully present mind, where you're grateful for everything you have, regardless of what happens. This is the ultimate key to unlocking your fullest potential. When you are able to adopt this mindfulness, loaded with gratitude and positive energy, it will allow you to be happier *right now*.

BUT SOME LITTLE THINGS DON'T MATTER

In the same way the little things in life can bring you joy and allow you to feel an immense amount of gratitude, there are some little things that just don't matter. The little things sometimes are just not worth it. Don't let your happiness today become collateral damage for your life happening the way it's supposed to. How many times do you go through your daily routine and allow something little annoy you? Let's say your coffee machine didn't function properly, or your dog got sick, or you there was a bunch of traffic on your way to work. Do you allow those mishaps to alter your state? Do those instances push you into a state of irritation and anger? This is what I mean when I say that the little things just don't matter. If your coffee machine broke down, if your dog puked, or if you had to detour on your way to work, let it be! Don't allow things out of your control to affect the positive energy you should be radiating throughout your day. Let these things come and go. Don't let the little things get in the way of yourself having a good, happy, fully present, and joyful day.

Just keep pushing forward, trusting the process, and adapting that attitude of gratitude we have been talking about. When you are in the correct frame of mind, radiating positive vibes, and seeing every crisis as a challenge, you're more likely to make the most out of your days. When compounded over time, this thought process is bound to help you make massive strides in your relative field.

Here's a tip that I have found useful in my own life. Start off your day with some empowering actions! What I have found helpful to incorporate into my daily morning routine is to spend some time sitting and being still—whether that be through guided meditation or just being in silence, focusing in on my inhale and exhale. I've found it tremendously supportive for my feelings of gratitude for everything I have in my life. Engaging in meditation and focusing on my breath helps me improve my attention to what matters.

As I sit in the mornings, I try to feel myself being in the present moment, nowhere but the "here and now." The value of being present, not thinking about past mistakes or worrying about what might happen in the future, is an unbelievable tool that can change your life. Just *be where your feet are.* Live in the moment and focus on the things you are grateful for, not the things that are out of your control that tend to cause you anxiety. That's where the meditation and practice of being in the moment helps improve your focus on the present. It's a fantastic method that helps you refresh your memory and brings everything that you have to be thankful, into the front of your mind. It focuses your attention *the positive*!

NO CONTINGENCY

Have you ever heard of destination addiction? This is the idea where you think you'll be happier once you finally receive whatever it is you are setting out to do or get. Whether that be a new car you've been thinking about, a desired salary of X amount of money per year, or that promotion that you think is coming your way. The truth is, having an attitude of gratitude is the key for what is going to catapult you to feeling happy and joyful *right now*, which should be all of our goals at the end of the day. No exceptions.

You want a bigger house? Great! That's a fantastic goal to shoot for. However, don't tell yourself that you will be happy once you finally sign the paperwork and obtain that goal. That's putting your happiness in external things. Joy is something you can create for yourself internally. Gratitude is about finding the balance, being content, and being grateful for what you have in your life right now. Not allowing your mood to be contingent on what happens that's out of your control. No contingencies.

Look at it this way. At least you have a roof over your head, a bed to sleep in, a fridge to keep your food in, and clean water! Can you see how you have so much around you that you can be grateful for? There are people in this world who don't know what they're going to do for their next meal, they don't know where they're going to sleep tonight, they don't know the next time they're going to get paid. Yet we're out here complaining that the wonderful life we're so blessed to live isn't good enough. Give me a break! We're blessed beyond comprehension. If you're alive, if you're breathing, if you're awake to experience the beauty of another day, be grateful for that. Not everyone has those same blessings, so it's vital to adapt an attitude of gratitude for those aspects of your life because they are not given and *should not be expected.*

> ## "Gratitude makes sense of our past, brings peace for today, and creates vision for tomorrow." —Melody Beattie

You need to try and embrace the grind. You need to try and love the life you are living today and every day. Love this part of your process. Love being the underdog and starting from where you are at now. Everything you are going through, or have yet to go through, needs to be seen as a part of the story. *Your* story. Feelings of joy will come to the surface if you can change your mindset and see your circumstances this way. You will see your emotions magnify as well when you overcome these challenging obstacles. You'll feel an *extra* sense of accomplishment when you persist and beat the odds to achieve something great.

Nonetheless, your desire to accomplish a heavy feat doesn't need to stop you from being happy and grateful right now! Of course, it will feel incredible once you are able to look back on your journey and see how far you've come. You'll soon look back on all of the trials that you've had to endure to get to where you wanted to go and be appreciative for those experiences. A remarkable flood of emotions will arise when you've become aware of all of the little things you have to be thankful for. Things that you've really had all along.

Everything happens for a reason. Our lives are fragile and even though the days seem to go by slowly at times, the years are flying by. Every moment we are on this planet, living our lives, should never be taken for granted because we have the privilege to experience the beautiful gift of what life really is. Be grateful for today and appreciate the endurance of the grind. Soon, you will encounter even more pleasure, knowing that you were resilient through all of the obstacles that were meant to throw you off track, all while maintaining a positive attitude and cultivating joy along the way. An attitude of gratitude will enhance the quality of your life and make you feel at peace with the present moment.

SMILE, LAUGH, LOVE.

As long as you follow the steps from the previous chapters of BTB, and you continue to engage with your habits and the process of winning each day as you go, you will reach your desired destination in due time. But loving the process and being grateful along the way will further enhance the experience of chasing down your dreams. So, smile today, laugh, send love out to a world that is starving for more of it. Radiate positive vibes and don't allow your joy to be contingent on the external. Be present for each part of the process and know that everything happens for good reason.

Learn from the best, have a compelling vision, practice the three D's, engage in powerful habits, fuel your confidence, be driven by your fears, don't make excuses, execute your game plan—all while being completely, fully present and grateful for the opportunity to keep pushing forward.

In the final chapter, I am going to dive into the common challenge many of us face in finding the balance between life and work. It's an enticing topic that I think is the perfect way to close off the book. We are almost there and we've covered some incredible topics. I'm thrilled to keep it going. Let's take that next, final step!

10

FINDING THE
BALANCE

As I've continued to grow throughout my life, the awareness that I am gaining on a day-to-day basis is truly remarkable. I'm starting to learn about what is really important to me and how I should allocate my time to best maximize the quality of my life. One of the most common struggles that many people face today, in a society consumed by work, is finding the balance between both.

Finding the balance is a collective issue dealt with by many individuals all across the globe. The difficulty lies in discovering what works best for you and then implementing that strategy into your life. We are constantly pulled in opposite directions though, making it feel almost impossible. As I have expanded cognizance, I've begun adopting a belief that a major component to personal happiness has to do with being able to find that balance. The balance of a weighted influence that identifies the proper proportions of time allocated to both life and work.

Finding the balance is a tough problem when looking for a one-size-fits-all solution because the answer varies completely on an individual basis. For me, I like to spend many hours of the day grinding away, improving my craft, while trying to aid my personal growth. Working more than the average person is what makes *me* happy and makes me feel fulfilled. It works for me, even though I still face challenges around the topic. That's not to say that the way I allocate my time and my idea of balance should be the same for everyone. But I truly believe that this constant battle of finding the balance in your own life and sticking to your unique layout and distribution of time, with complete contentment, is a significant element to living a joyful lifestyle.

I can sit here preaching all day long, telling you to go and learn from the best, develop your vision, follow the three D's, have good habits, etc., etc., etc. I would be doing each and every single person reading this book an injustice if I didn't remind them about the principle of balance.

In my personal life, I've found this to be fundamental to my own happiness. As an individual, I strive to do incredible things, which leads me to constantly focus on the future. I'm always working towards building and creating my vision and I do it to such an intense degree that sometimes it removes me from the present. My drive tends to take me out of the moment. I'm not proud of the fact that I struggle to with this and I don't like that it's hard for me at times to enjoy the beautiful things that this life provides me.

What do you think most people are searching for in their quest to fulfill their potential? If you really had to narrow it down, what is the simplest answer? Money? Fame? Power? Maybe... but have you ever thought that everyone is just trying their best to be happy? To do what will fulfill them? Because at the end of the day, that's all that we want, isn't it? To be happy... content... proud... joyful...

Happiness. What does that mean and how do you get it? The answer differs and is distinct to each individual, but the questions you need to ask yourself are:

- What matters to me?
- What's important to me in my life?
- What do I want out of the precious time I have on Earth?

Finding the balance is an essential principle to finding that happiness that you're looking for. Everything we do in life is about finding the balance!

A few years back, I was scrolling through social media, going through my feed, and I came across a quote from Ray Lewis that really struck home for me. Ray Lewis is a Hall of Fame American football player who has built a reputation as one of the meanest competitors to ever take the football field. Before seeing this quote by him, I had always imagined him as an absolute work horse. One of those special individuals who holds a high value to the man who is always working. The players who are always grinding and putting in a shift. I previously thought he would have attributed his success, maybe, to his mindset and relentless drive and dedication. A man who had a long sustaining career in the NFL, including multiple personal accolades and team trophies. After discovering what he had to say about our society and finding the balance, my perspective on the topic was forever changed...

> **"We need to stop glorifying the person who works
> all weekend and rather praise the person who succeeds
> in finding the balance between work, family, and rest.
> Our culture of celebrating the workaholic is one of the main
> reasons we are seeing an increase in mental, emotional,
> and physical burnout."** —Ray Lewis

DIVERSIFY

An incredibly interesting perspective, don't you think? Grind and then work, work and then grind, grind and then work some more. I live this way myself and it's how I operate the majority of the time. I feel like work is just inscribed in my DNA. It's hard for me to escape it and get away. Working towards my dream was all I knew, and it's still all I know! I still haven't even taken a vacation and I've been in the league for years! Although hard work is an indispensable part of the puzzle to success, it needs to be allocated to different areas of your life. Just like how in investing they say diversification is the most important trait to long-term success, so is the diversification of your work into the portfolio that is your life. Because work shouldn't just be thought of as your job—what you do from 9–5. To work hard in the office is one thing, but what happens when you clock out and go home for the rest of the day? As life continues, it's not like you can just turn off the need to work and disregard the rest of your responsibilities, right?

We all have goals and roles that need to be played in our day-to-day life. Think about it. You still have to go home and work. You have to work on your relationship with your significant other, you may have to cook to put dinner on the table for your family. You have to continue to work on yourself to be the best father or mother for you children that you can be. It's all work. We just need to learn how to allocate it and still take care of ourselves.

Working hard is not only about earning a ridiculous amount of wealth, or whatever else you associate to working. An overlooked category of work comes across in your relationships and yourself! Because that, in itself, is *hard work!* If you are to maintain a healthy marriage or continue nourishing empowering relationships with your close ones, you have to work hard in those areas too! Relationships require work. Raising kids requires work. Cooking, cleaning, and maintaining your house requires work. Bettering yourself so that you can be a better person for those around you requires *work.* Again, our lives are encompassed around the idea of working. Work, work, work. Everything in our world today revolves around work, and that can be overwhelming. So how do we find the balance?

SELF-CARE

One of the hardest things to do in our lifetime is to find that perfect balance between life and work. How do we find the balance between chasing down our greatest desires while being content with where we are and what we have? How do we make sure we're not running ourselves into the ground and burning ourselves out? How do we make sure that after a long day, week, month, or year, we come back the next even hungrier? How do we refresh ourselves and recharge our batteries? This is all a part of *finding the balance.*

I believe this idea of balance plays an extremely important role in my life and in my career. My levels of engagement and my discipline in my routines is crazy. I spend a ridiculous amount of emotional, mental, and physical energy on the game that I love. I invest myself to the highest order, which might not always be the best thing. With that being said, I've found it awfully important to find the balance between being disciplined and dedicated to my career, while being present in the moment and giving myself time to enjoy this precious life that we are living.

I've personally struggled with finding the balance throughout my playing career because any time I engage in activities that I feel will not help me get to where I want to go, I feel an undeniable wave of guilt. A guilt that's passing along the message that I'm cheating myself. If I were to eat a cheat meal, take a day off to rest, or relax with my friends and family, there was a time where I felt like I was cheating myself. I could literally, physically, feel the strongest sensations of guilt running throughout my body. Sometimes I would even lose sleep.

I think many individuals who are naturally future-focused, determined to reach their goals, and motivated to acquire the things they desire, all face similar internal battles with themselves. I always feel like I could be doing more, so when I choose to take time off and enjoy a night with my family and friends, or choose to have a cheat meal, I feel that these instances can serve as possible evidence against myself. That indication causes me to think very negatively, and the way I represent those events to myself is that they prove that I don't want my long-term goals as much as I had once thought I did.

As good as it is to be disciplined, as good as it is and to be hard on yourself by holding yourself to the highest standard, it can be detrimental at the same time. Feeling guilt so intensely that, for example, it causes me to lose sleep, is obviously not healthy or good for my overall wellbeing.

When you struggle to find the balance in your life, you are going to end up hitting a wall at some point and your mental and emotional capacity will take a toll. You will find it tremendously difficult to be in the here and now. You won't be able to cultivate joy in the present moment.

LIVE!

Here is a situation that my wife always is able to revert to that helps us enjoy *today*. Due to the most unfortunate of situations where she lost her father when was only 10 years old, her perspective and advice helped me, specifically, find more balance in life. She often tells me about stories about how her father always lived his life to the fullest. He was happy, caring, and always could be found in good spirit. He lived for *"today."* If he wanted to do something, he did it. Now, because of what happened directly to her and her family, she is able to find that balance a bit easier than I can because of the severity of her experience. She's always the first to remind me that tomorrow is not promised! And it isn't... So, don't rob yourself of too much joy today. Partake in activities that bring you true joy and fill your heart. Finding that balance away from work will allow you to recharge, refuel, and come back to work feeling more refreshed than ever before! Discipline and dedication will bring you towards your goals, but don't forget to live a little either. Because you also don't want to look back and regret having *not* lived your life.

The Dalai Lama, when asked what surprised him most about humanity, answered:

> *"Man! Because he sacrifices his health in order to make money. Then he sacrifices money to recuperate his health. And then he is so anxious about the future that he does not enjoy the present; the result being that he does not live in the present or the future; he lives as if he is never going to die, and then dies having never really lived."*

Let us receive life's most precious gift! That of finding the proper balance between our work and our lives. I don't want to go to my grave with having never lived, and neither should you! The moments of loosening up your bolts allow you to refuel, refocus, and realign yourself with what really matters. These instances allow you to enjoy your life in a world that is so consumed by work. I'm advising you, solely from personal experience because in my line of work, this principle has especially become a chief concept that I've been working towards implementing into my life.

Finding the proper balance will further push me through the long grueling months of a professional soccer season, fighting against the possibility of burning myself out. I don't want to be on my deathbed someday having never enjoyed my life, especially considering how fast the years are passing me by. I'm grateful to be here, living my life with my friends and family as well. Let us harvest that beauty and enjoy the gift of life that we have received today because tomorrow is never guaranteed!

Throughout the ups and downs, the highs and the lows, and the emotional waves of my career, I have learned that there are times that can be very draining—particularly when the end goal that you desire and long for is wanted so badly! Try and find it within yourself to let go and find the balance between your work and your life. As long as you try to work your hardest and you are dedicated and committed throughout the weeks, months, and years, you owe it to yourself to allot some time to relax and put your attention elsewhere.

Work hard and earn it because you deserve it!

I know it sounds odd, but this will actually help you down the road in the long-term because it will allow you to stay focused and absorbed with what you are doing for a longer period of time without feeling drained. As long as the activities you are engaging in aren't overboard and are taking up your time for the better of your well-being, so be it! Send it! *Don't forget to live!*

YOUR ACTION ITEM. Some activities that I have found enjoyable that help me relax a little and get my mind away from the game can vary from things like playing golf, going out to dinner with my wife, grabbing a cup of coffee with a friend, going for evening walks in nature, or taking my dog to the park. What are some things you would like to do that will help you practice balance in your life? What have you been refraining from doing that you have been dying to do? Find the balance and write down three things that you are going to start doing to help you absorb the beauty of life and live it to the fullest. Are you going dedicate yourself to having a cheat meal every week? Play golf once a week? Take your kids to the park or out for ice cream? These activities can be whatever you want! Get creative and make sure you practice them!

1.

2.

3.

CHALLENGES

As I continue to learn on a day-to-day basis, I continue to struggle with finding the balance fully, up until this very day. A challenge that I've come to notice is that when I'm searching for activities and things that bring me joy, most of the time they revert back to my obsession with learning. The majority of these practices align with my hunger to better myself as a person, or a footballer.

I've found the profession of professional soccer, although it has always been my dream and is an absolute privilege, to be awfully hard on me at times because I don't take losses well. When we lose a game, I typically tend to lose a lot of sleep, overthinking many actions from the game, and analyzing where I could have done better. I find those constant thoughts exhausting because it's so difficult for me to turn them off.

In football, when you prepare all week during practice with the main purpose of trying to get the win on the weekend, two things can happen. Obviously, we either can win or lose that game. The week that follows after a victory is typically fantastic. Everyone is happy at the training facility. The vibes in the locker room are positive and training seems to run smoother than ever. However, this is a game of extremes and the contrary is also, unfortunately, true. When you prepare all week during practice and then lose that game, the vibe is much worse, and that cycle of negative emotions can be taxing over a season that runs for 10+ months. The same can be true for you in your job as well. Whether you just landed that new client, just closed on a deal, or just got a promotion. You can also marginally miss landing that new client, or watch a deal fall through. Therefore, this process of going through intense ups and downs can be taxing on an individual. You can become emotionally expended and mentally depleted if you don't find ways to find balance!

I feel like the process is magnified for myself because I care so much. Maybe *too* much. I'm thinking nearly 24/7 on straight football and on my career. Always thinking about what I could be doing better to give myself that much more of a chance to succeed. It really is a struggle and can take a toll on my emotions if I don't find a way to put them in check.

Finding the balance is so important. In fact, its importance cannot be undermined. You don't want to let a bad training session, a bad day at work, or tough day in the office bleed into the rest of your life. To the point where you come home after work or practice and are giving the cold shoulder to your wife because you had a rough day on the job. The consequence of not being able to find that balance can be destructive to your emotional well-being, and not only to yourself, but to those around you as well. You don't want to let those struggles propel you to neglect your family and friends because you're too consumed with working.

I encourage you to constantly try and find the balance between your life and your work, which has proven itself to be a never-ending search. Just try and remain consistent in your habits. Even though the BTB lifestyle revolves around learning from the best, implementing the three D's, not making excuses etc., don't forget to live your life as well. To enjoy your family, to show appreciation for your loved ones, and to be grateful for everything you have *right now*. Having a positive attitude and an attitude of gratitude is what will further assist you in finding the balance. The one that is so hard to find. I still struggle with it to this day, but I couldn't not mention it in this book because of how important it is to BTB.

One thing I can promise you though is that when you do find that balance, your life will be much more fulfilling, and you will actually find yourself performing better both at your job and in your daily life as a person because your levels of happiness will increase. We all know our capacities to perform are always elevated when we are mentally in a good place.

THE GROUNDWORK

Ultimately, the goal of this portion of the book is to heighten your ability to find the balance between your work and your life. How we think about balance and how we manage, perceive, and handle what goes on in our daily lives is rooted into our philosophies and understandings of ourselves. How each of us lives is based off of our paradigms, perspectives, and interpretations. Many times, these are shaped from our own experiences and inscribed into our hardwiring. We live according to our own beliefs as to how we should do things because we just don't know anything else.

I would like to provide some food for thought. A little background knowledge about philosophy that may help change the way you think and view your life. To start, I would like to take us back in time in order to discover some of the differences and similarities between the roots of philosophy, which lie in the regional categories of Eastern and Western thinking. I truly believe that these ideas can give you the foundation you need to find balance in your life.

First and foremost, lets define philosophy. Generally, it is *"the study of wisdom or knowledge about the general problems, facts, and situations connected with human existence, values, reasons, and general reality."* The basis of philosophy is to seek responses, reasons, and answers to our life occurrences and their factors. Summing up our underlying motives to act and respond to what happens in our lives. All of it—the way we think, the way we act/react, comes down to the root of our thoughts and our basis of philosophy.

I think there is something extremely interesting, and quite beautiful actually, about philosophy and its role in our societies today. Recently, I came across an article on **theschooloflife.com**, whose articles and teachings are based after *"The Book of Life."* This framework and its philosophies were learned from the one and only, Lao Tzu. I found these lessons to be immensely moving and impactful. These articles highlight some of the main ideas and crucial points of philosophy, and I want to share them with you briefly as well because I believe they play an important role in BTB.

"All of humanity's problems stem from man's inability to sit quietly in a room alone." —Blaise Pascal

PHILOSOPHICAL THINKING

Philosophy is an interesting concept because the term can seem a bit intimidating. The study of philosophy is aimed towards an overlying purpose. One that wishes to make us wiser, while allowing us to live less agitated, but more thoughtful lives. By keeping this framework at the front of our focus, we will then be more open to the idea of appreciation for all that we have.

> **"The wise person should take care to grow completely at home with the ordinary shambles of existence. By keeping the dark backdrop of life always in his mind, he sharpened his appreciation of whatever stood out against it."** —The School of Life

The point of growing at home with the shambles of existence reiterates the importance of being happy with the simple fact that we are here, and we are alive. Some people didn't receive that same blessing today. If you opened your eyes this morning, if you are healthy, alive, and breathing, you have every right to feel extremely grateful for another day and another opportunity to be here, today.

Notice how the focus on what is important is not necessarily anything material. The idea and value of happiness is not encapsulated in our jobs and doesn't require any hands-on work or in striving to reach immense levels of success. Rather, happiness is just capturing the beautiful sense of being, mastering your spiritual self, and being fulfilled by solely being alive. The article says "by keeping the dark backdrop of life always in his mind"—a seemingly dark message, but one that's extremely powerful in redefining what we value in our lives. Remembering that tomorrow isn't promised; therefore, be happy to be alive. Growing content with solely existing, both for yourself and your family, is in itself, a reason to be thankful.

> ## "Philosophy is a discipline committed to helping us
> ## to live wiser and less sorrowful lives." —Lao Tzu

Lao Tzu describes Wu Wei (the Chinese term at the heart of Daoism) as *"not making an effort, going with the flow,"* but it doesn't in any way imply laziness or sloth. Instead, it suggests that we may be powerless to alter certain events, but we remain free to choose our attitude towards them. Choosing our feelings about certain events, rather than letting them control us. We are always in control, but first we must learn to master ourselves and the ways we choose to think.

For some books regarding philosophy, spirituality, meditations, presence, and flow, you can find my favorites, again, on the **BTB Website**. Some of my top recommendations would be *"The Seven Spiritual Laws of Success"* by Deepak Chopra, *"Meditations"* by Marcus Aurelius, *"The Tao of Pooh"* by Benjamin Hoff, *"A Master's Secret Whispers"* by Kapil Gupta, and *"Stillness is the Key"* by Ryan Holiday.

> ## "Sitting alone' doesn't mean literally being on the bed,
> ## but rather staying undistracted with ourselves:
> ## appreciating small pleasures; examining the contents of
> ## our own minds; allowing the quieter (but important) part
> ## of our psyche to emerge; thinking before we act.
> ## We shall learn how to become better friends to ourselves."
> —The School of Life

As I've talked about finding the motivation and inspiration within yourself to create everlasting success, I believe that finding this balance is the true key to personal wealth. Reading books on the pertaining categories, via learning from the best, has really catapulted me towards trying to find that balance more often in my life. I believe that these practices and ways of thinking have truly improved the quality of my life and have allowed me to be happier on a day-to-day basis. Philosophy highlights that success is spiritual and is achieved when one learns to conquer themselves.

What an interesting perspective! It's crazy because so many of the things I've touched on throughout this book bring me back to this main idea, that everything in life has to do with how we think. It all starts with our minds and our mentalities.

Many of us struggle to sit alone with our own thoughts. We crave distraction. We crave that mini dopamine hit that's released when we scroll our Instagram or Twitter feed. Look around the next time you're in the line at Starbucks and observe how many people are lost in the digital world, not truly experiencing life as it is. It's all a distraction and it's something we've trained ourselves to need. Anytime we're waiting or have some down time, many of us chose to spend it distracting ourselves from our own thoughts.

As long as we allow our subconscious thoughts to be in control, we'll never be able to find true balance. It starts in controlling our beliefs, altering our judgments, and becoming masters of our own minds. If you can control how you think and come to a true understanding of yourself, you're bound to live a life of joy, prosperity, and abundance. Success is waiting for you. It's all there for the taking, right behind the door of self-mastery.

We need to befriend ourselves and be compassionate towards our thoughts, understanding then that we have the power to control them. We have the capability to manage our own thoughts and how we react to certain events or circumstances. These thoughts and responses can govern the internal feelings that you have about yourself and can be instrumental in finding *your* desired balance between life and work.

I think studying philosophy can be an interesting endeavor if you want to learn more about it. I encourage you to dive into it a bit! I've found it extremely helpful in my own life, to step away from work and find contentment with the way things are in my life, right now. That's not to say that I'm complacent or not hungry to achieve my goals, but rather it's allowing me to love *this part of the process*. To be thankful for where I'm at today and to be grateful for what I have.

LOVE YOURSELF

You may be asking why I am sharing all of this with you. All of this nonsense about philosophy? You bought this book to learn how to BTB, how to become the best version of yourself, defy limitations and maximize your potential. However, understanding the methodology rooted in this philosophy can bring serious happiness to your life right now! Because a lot of you are looking for more, striving for more, hungry for more... when everything you really need you may already have. I want to encourage the idea that evolving your life around destination-oriented happiness will lead you to a path of complete sorrow. It will leave you feeling empty, without enjoying the truest fruits that life has to offer.

> **"If you want to improve your self-worth, stop giving other people the calculator."** —Tim Fargo

There are people out there with all the money in the world—millions and even billions of dollars, private jets, vacation homes, a mansion with 10-car garages, basketball courts—but they are still empty inside because they haven't mastered or filled the voids in their hearts with true love and compassion for themselves. They haven't mastered the art of being content with their lives. They haven't adopted the practices of gratitude or learned how to be appreciative for everything they have, and that as Tony Robbins said, is an absolute shame!

Being able to sit with your own thoughts, recenter yourself, and realign your focus on what really matters... is the key my friends. Stillness, being, existence, presence... Happiness is internal, and it starts with looking inwards and becoming comfortable with who you are and finding the balance between being content with what you have, but also striving for more. Being able to work hard in order to create the life you desire is necessary if you want to accomplish more, but to be present along the way and love every step of the process is, what I would call, true happiness. That is our world's greatest gift, and that is what you should be aiming for. To learn more about how to fall in love with the process of becoming great while harvesting this concept. I'd really recommend you take a look at *"Chop Wood Carry Water"* by Joshua Medcalf. Really good book if you're looking for another way to *learn from the best*!

> **"Most people chase success at work, thinking that will make them happy. The truth is that happiness at work will make you successful."** —Alexander Kjerulf

You may be stressed, overwhelmed, and on the brink of burning out physically and mentally. As we come to a close, allow me to touch on one of the final pieces to promote finding the balance. Recentering yourself.

RECENTER

You can try various practices that may help you in recentering yourself. First, put your phone down, close your email, and shut your laptop. Try sitting outside and just appreciating the beauty of nature, be aware of your breath, inhale gratitude, meditate, and become whole with yourself.

Too often, we are lured by external things that are constantly fighting for our attention and taking us away from the present. Even though many of these events require your attention, you must not forget to come back to the here and now.

The key to happiness is finding the equilibrium between being future focused and being present. This idea, I believe, is a principle for finding real happiness and true wealth. Not just something to try and apply if you want to make millions of dollars. If you are striving the be the best version of yourself, you will notice how crucial it is to find the balance in your life. Not to neglect and miss the beauty that is here today because you're too focused on tomorrow.

BTB CONCLUSION

Congratulations! You've successfully covered and made it through all the steps to incorporate and adopt the BTB lifestyle. I hope you have picked up many tips and pieces of advice that can help you better the quality of your life moving forward.

As I have gotten older, even though I'm writing this in my early twenties and the days continue to pass me by, I am discovering new things and gaining a sublime level of consciousness and clarity about what it really means to be happy, alive, and self-aware. I've stepped into a mind frame where my mission to prosper and be all I can be is so strong that I can bring joy to myself and those around me.

My purpose for writing this book is to help anyone and everyone who has dreams of becoming something more, to encourage anyone who refuses to believe and live up to the limitations pressed on them by society, and to support anyone striving to reach their maximum potential. My slogan, and the phrase that I attribute my life to, is to always BE THE BEST. To strive for nothing more and nothing less.

I'm not talking about becoming the best player, writer, teacher or leader to ever walk the face of the Earth. Not the richest or the wealthiest. Not the most valuable or the most successful person the world has ever seen. But to *BTB*. Be the best version of *yourself*.

What do *you* want out of life and what is the reason behind it? No one can tell you how to be happy. It doesn't say anywhere in the manual of life that you need to make a certain amount of money or reach a certain level of success to be happy, does it? At the end of the day, that's what we are all after here, isn't it? The wholesome feeling of joy and prosperity in all aspects of your life. To feel that sense of fulfillment.

I want to inspire you to be the best version of yourself every day, and to find absolute bliss in the process which can ultimately lead you to something you never could have dreamt of. I want to help you open your eyes and see the potential you have that already lies within.

"Trust the wait. Embrace the uncertainty. Enjoy the beauty of becoming. When nothing is certain, anything is possible."
—Mandy Hale

With relentless dedication and passion for what you are doing, with hard work executed over an extended period of time, with a whole lot of patience and intentional practice, good things *will* come! I want to show everyone what can be possible when you follow the tactics and principles that I have laid out throughout this book, which I have seen work in the many aspects of my life and along the journey I have been on—more often than not.

In life, there are no guarantees. You have to be willing to live boldly and act in spite of your fear and in spite of the possibility of failure. The days go by slowly while the years seem to pass us by faster than the shooting stars we saw as kids. The life that we are living today, in this very moment, is a blessed one. Start to shift your perception and you will see how amazing and blessed you are *right now*.

With that being said, I want to invite you to join me on a quest to be the best version of yourself every day, and every moment that you are alive, because this life is a gift, and we only get to live it once.

I don't have all the answers, and I am not claiming to know everything. I'm also not saying that this is the one and only way for any individual to achieve success. I am just speaking from my own personal experiences, my own perspective, and the lessons I have learned along the way. I wanted to share with you the tactics that have worked best for me. The ones that I have accumulated from so many years on this constant grind of obsessing over personally growing and trying to achieve my full potential.

This is book is based on what has come through years of experimenting—reading books, listening to podcasts, online courses, masterclasses, conversations with mentors and those who've reached abundant success, and most importantly, my personal experiences and what I have seen work in my own life. My goal is to help inspire and show anyone who is looking for a deeper purpose and has the self-belief deep inside themselves that they were born to do something great.

One thing I know for certain is that I will never stop learning. I will never be complacent and content with where I am. I will always shoot to improve. To develop. To be better that I was yesterday. I am addicted with learning new things and striving to be the best I can be.

I hope you can take away what you like from this book and leave behind the things you don't. BTB isn't only an approach, a method, or a promise, but a lifestyle. I can't wait to see what you can do when you apply these principles to your life. You'll be amazed to see what is waiting for you on the other side of committing yourself to being the best. I'm here for you if you need anything or having any questions. I'm excited to follow your journey and I'll be here to support you, every step of the way.

This is all coming from an average kid from Schaumburg, IL who had a dream to play professional soccer. Who played in the streets growing up with friends, on turf fields by my house where my parents would watch from their lawn chairs. Who had a vision of scoring goals in stadiums in front of thousands of fans and feeling that adrenaline rush as I celebrated in an empty field at a park in my neighborhood. Who desired to inspire. Who developed good, empowering habits years ago and has been disciplined enough to trust the process all the way through. And I'm still going. I've got my aim higher than ever to continue to strive to be the best version of myself and I'm excited to see what I can accomplish.

When you put this book down, I want you to walk away with one thing and one thing only. Make me a promise that from this day forward, you're going to *Bet On Yourself*. Every. Single. Day. Against all odds. You can do it. I believe in you.

Build unshakeable confidence. Tune out the noise. Rise to the occasion.

Thank you for taking the time to read this. I know how valuable your time is and it means the world to me that you made the decision to pick up and read my book. Take the first step! I invite you all to join the movement.

"You can teach a student a lesson for a day; but if you can teach him to learn by creating curiosity, he will continue the learning process for as long as he lives." —Clay P. Bedford

This is a way of life. This is a lifestyle. This is a mindset. Take it upon yourself. #BTB.

BIBLIOGRAPHY
References, Resources, & Recommended Reading

BOOKS:

1. **The Compound Effect**, Darren Hardy
Hardy, Darren. *The Compound Effect*. Boston, MA, Da Capo Press, 2010.

2. **Awaken The Giant Within**, Tony Robbins
Robbins, Anthony. *Awaken the Giant Within*. New York, NY, Simon & Schuster Paperbacks, 1991.

3. **Relentless: Good to Great to Unstoppable**, Tim Grover
Grover, Tim. *Relentless: Good to Great to Unstoppable*. New York, NY, Simon & Schuster Paperbacks, 2013.

4. **The 5 A.M. Club**, Robin Sharma
Sharma, Robin. *The 5 A.M. Club*. Toronto, Ontario, Canada, HarperCollins Publishers Ltd., 2018.

5. **The 15 Invaluable Laws of Growth**, John C. Maxwell
Maxwell, John C. *The 15 Invaluable Laws of Growth*. Center Street Publishing, 2012.

6. **Chop Wood**, Carry Water, Joshua Medcalf
Medcalf, Joshua. *Chop Wood*, Carry Water. Joshua Medcalf, 2015.

7. **The Seven Habits of Highly Effective People**, Stephen Covey
Covey, Stephen. *The Seven Habits of Highly Effective People*. New York, NY, Simon & Schuster Paperbacks, 1989.

8. **Atomic Habits**, James Clear
Clear, James. *Atomic Habits*. New York, NY, Penguin Random House LLC, 2018.

9. **It's All In Your Head**, Russ Vitale,
Russ. *It's All In Your Head*. New York, NY, HarperCollins Publishers Ltd., 2019.

10. **Can't Hurt Me**, David Goggins
Goggins, David. *Can't Hurt Me*. Lioncrest Publishing, 2018.

11. **Start With Why**, Simon Sinek
Sinek, Simon. *Start With Why*. New York, NY, The Penguin Group, 2009.

12. **Mind Gym**, Gary Mack
Mack, Gary. *Mind Gym*. New York, NY, McGraw-Hill, 2001.

13. **Stillness Is The Key**, Ryan Holiday
Holiday, Ryan. *Stillness Is The Key*. New York, NY, Portfolio/Penguin, 2019.

14. **The Seven Spiritual Laws of Success**, Deepak Chopra
Chopra, Deepak. *The Seven Spiritual Laws of Success*. San Rafael, CA. Novato, CA, Amber-Allen Publishing, New World Library, 1994.

15. **Innercise**, John Assaraf
Assaraf, John. *Innercise: The New Science to Unlock Your Brain's Hidden Power*. Cardiff, CA, Waterside Press, 2018.

16. **A Master's Secret Whispers**, Kapil Gupta
Gupta, Kapil. *A Master's Secret Whispers*. Kapil Gupta, 2017.

17. **13 Things Mentally Strong People Don't Do**, Amy Morin
Morin, Amy. *13 Things Mentally Strong People Don't Do*. New York, NY, HarperCollins, 2014.

18. **Meditations**, Marcus Aurelius
Aurelius, Marcus. *Meditations*. Toronto, Canada, Modern Library Random House, 2003.

19. **Deep Work**, Cal Newport
Newport, Cal. *Deep Work*. New York, NY, Grand Central Publishing, 2016.

20. **Think And Grow Rich**, Napoleon Hill
Hill, Napoleon. *Think and Grow Rich*. United Kingdom, England, The Penguin Group, 1937.

ARTICLES:

1. *"Six Ideas from Eastern Philosophy."* The School of Life. https://www.theschooloflife.com/thebookoflife/six-ideas-from-eastern-philosophy/

2. *"Six Ideas from Western Philosophy."* The School of Life. https://www.theschooloflife.com/thebookoflife/six-ideas-from-western-philosophy/

BTB WEBSITE:
www.bethebest-btb.com

FOLLOW ME:
On Twitter & Instagram:
@cmueller1662

PODCASTS:
The Ed Mylett Show

ACKNOWLEDGMENTS

I need to thank God, first and foremost, for the unbelievable things He's done in my life. Without my faith serving as my foundation throughout my journey, I wouldn't be where I am, or who I am today. God has blessed me beyond belief and has afforded me the privilege of living out my dream.

To my wife, Alyssa, who has unconditionally supported me, cared for me, and believed in me since we were 16 years old. You've been with me from the start and I couldn't thank you enough for being my life companion, my best friend, and for inspiring me to be the best version of myself every day.

To my family, who've provided me with unwavering love and given me the opportunities to grow into the person I am today. Thank you for your endless care and support.

Made in the USA
Coppell, TX
11 December 2021